ROYAL FESTIVAL

CENTRE POINT

WATERLOO AIR TERMINAL

MODERN LONDON

Lukas Novotny

Lukas Novotny

MODERN LONDON

An illustrated cityscape from
the 1920s to the present day

WHITE LION
PUBLISHING

The Beginning

Modern London tells the story of how London, a seemingly untameable tangle of a city, became modern. It's an intriguing tale of struggle between the long-held and esteemed architectural traditions of the island nation and the inescapable influences of modern American and European design. Divided into decades, a century of evolution from the 1920s to the present day is explored through the illustration of dozens of notable buildings; an eclectic mix of popular landmarks, demolished masterpieces and forgotten oddities. Each are placed in their wider cultural context by technological and transport innovations of the time.

Unlike New York with its patchwork grid, and Paris with its long, tree-lined boulevards, London is not the result of a grand plan – it was (and still is) shaped by invisible and often contradictory forces. The pace of change of the cityscape is ever increasing, and so it's now more important than ever to understand how London came to look as it does today. Reading this book might not only help you understand the capital's history and present-day visage, but also give you clues as to its architectural future.

The shadows of enemy airships gliding ominously through London's night sky may be a thing of the past. But at the dawn of the 1920s, the Great War – which took 16 million lives and left the European continent devastated – is just two years gone. Nevertheless, London, the largest city in the world at the time, has been left more or less unscathed, its economy in fact prospering from the development of arms factories and the rise of female employment. As war restrictions are lifted, the West End lights up with new night clubs and jazz bars. At the same time, big aristocratic mansions make way for grand new hotels hoping to attract the custom of wealthy Americans. A change is in the air.

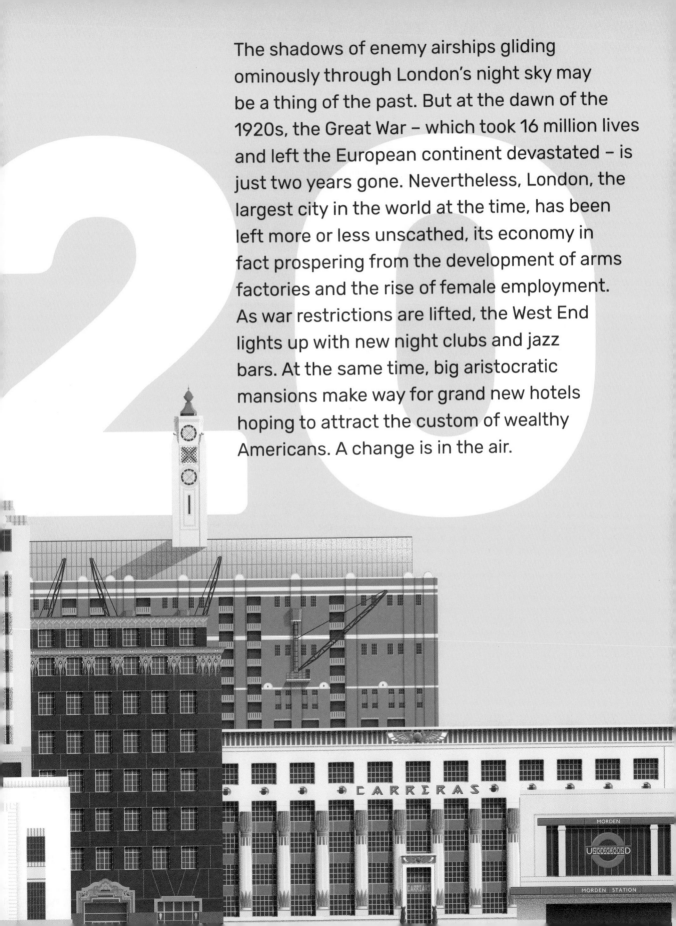

In the 1920s, London's large customer base, relatively cheap labour and docks linked by ship to cities around the world made it an ideal location for manufacturing. Emerging American companies soon set up shop, and aspiring British businesses looked up to these overseas corporations and their practices. Architecture soon became a method of advertisement. Confident and bold façades competed for attention and paid little mind to the opinions of critics.

A perfect example of this is the **Carreras Black Cat Cigarette Factory (001)** in Camden. Following the discovery of the intact tomb of Tutankhamun in 1923, the British public had become obsessed with ancient Egypt and everything to do with it; Egyptian motifs started to appear on new buildings across the capital.

Carreras' bosses liked the idea, and decided to take it one step further. The façade of their new factory would come to resemble an ancient Egyptian temple. Painted in bright colours, covered from head to toe with Egyptian décor and guarded by two sculpted cat-gods, it certainly attracted the attention of the public. To ensure that nobody missed the trick, an extravagant opening day saw the streets around the factory transformed into an African desert scene. The pavements were buried in sand and processions of actors in Egyptian costumes streamed through the streets. They even staged a chariot race.

But just ten years later, when the threat of Nazi occupation loomed large, certain people worried that the winged sun motif adorning the façade too closely resembled the Nazi eagle, and it was swiftly covered up. In 1961, when the factory was converted into offices, the Egyptian style had long gone out of fashion and all the decoration was chiselled away. Even the round columns were boxed, to give the building a more modern appearance. In the 1990s, however, people came to appreciate the style once again. The building was renovated and most of the original decoration restored, although the winged sun motif didn't come back.

 001 **Carreras Black Cat Cigarette Factory**
M.E. & O.H. Collins with A.G. Porri
🕐 1928   📍 NW1 7AW

Firestone Factory
Wallis, Gilbert and Partners

🕐 1928 🗓 1980 📍 TW7 5QD

Police Box Mark 2

685 sturdy concrete boxes situated across London worked as a direct telephone connection to a police station. They first appeared in 1929 in a design by Gilbert Mackenzie Trench. The box gained international fame thanks to the *Doctor Who* television series, in which it featured as a time machine.

Among the numerous American corporations competing for space in the city was the Ohio-based Firestone Tire and Rubber Company. A factory was built on the Great West Road, which soon became a hotspot for overseas businesses. The **Firestone Factory (002)** was designed by Wallis, Gilbert and Partners – itself a partnership between an American construction company and an English architect. It was built with incredible speed – from drawing board to finished building it took a mere twenty-one weeks. The façade's composition and decoration was once again inspired by ancient Egypt, although it was far more restrained than that of the Carreras factory.

In 1980, due to high wage costs, industrial unrest and high prices caused by the oil crisis, the factory workers were laid off and the land was sold to a developer. Both the local council and the Department of the Environment worked hard to get the building listed, but the developer Victor Matthews soon got wind of this and ordered its quick demolition. It was destroyed over the August bank holiday weekend, two days before the building was due to be listed – and saved. The demolition was a nasty shock to many and it accelerated efforts to protect other industrial landmarks, such as the Hoover Building (018).

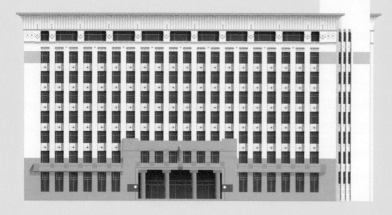

(003) **Adelaide House**
John J. Burnet & Thomas S. Tait
🕓 1925 📍 EC4R 9HA ↕ 43M

New office buildings of successful British corporations and banks rose up all around the financial district of London, commonly known as the City (note the capital 'c'). The most modern was **Adelaide House (003)**, designed by Scottish architects John J. Burnet and Thomas S. Tait. Both had travelled to the US before, with Tait working for a short time in New York City; their travels were to have a noticeable influence on the finished building. When it opened in 1925, it became the tallest – and most modern – office building in London. It was the first office block to have a steel frame, central ventilation and a telephone connection on every floor. There was even a fruit garden and an eighteen-hole mini golf course on the roof. The façade incorporates a mixture of American modernism and, of course, ancient Egyptian motifs.

Later, Tait joined forces with Irishman Charles Ernest Elcock, to design the **Daily Telegraph Building (004)**. It was situated on Fleet Street, home to many national newspapers. The basement contained the printing presses, while offices and flats occupied the floors above. The building was surprisingly modern, considering its conservative client. The façade and interior are rich in detail, and clearly influenced by the American Art Deco style that was popular during the period.

Assisting with exterior decoration was the sculptor Samuel Rabinovitch (who also worked on 55 Broadway (008)). He carved his odd sculptures directly into the façade, perched on scaffolding. This was to be his last sculpting project before he left the arts for professional wrestling. He won a bronze medal at the 1928 Olympics in Amsterdam.

(004) **Daily Telegraph Building**
Thomas S. Tait &
Charles Ernest Elcock
🕓 1928 📍 EC4A 2BJ

Armstrong Whitworth Argosy II

This twenty-seat airplane operated from Croydon Airport. It mainly flew the busiest air route of the time, from London to Paris. One mysteriously crashed in 1933 on its way to London. Strangely, one passenger – a German dentist – jumped out before the crash (without a parachute), leading some to believe he sabotaged the plane.

Meanwhile, in south London, **Croydon Airport Terminal (005)** opened. The actual airfield was established in 1915, as a protection against Zeppelin airships bombing the city. It was also the site of Winston Churchill's horrific plane crash in 1919, in which he almost died in a failed attempt to obtain a pilot's licence. Since then, it had evolved into the first international passenger airport in Britain. The ultra-modern control tower, part of a new terminal, was the first in the world and became a model for new airports worldwide.

The concept and equipment were brand new, but the architecture remained classical, although its minimal décor and high-tech antennas on the rooftop made for a modern appearance. The airport was frequented by many famous aviators and celebrities in the interwar years. Charles Lindbergh even stopped by after becoming the first pilot to fly over the Atlantic Ocean. He was welcomed by a 100,000-strong crowd.

(005) **Croydon Airport Terminal**
Architects of Air Ministry
🕐 1928   📍 CR0 0XZ

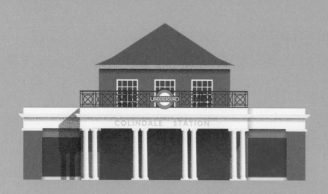

 Colindale Station
Stanley Heaps

🕐 1924   ⬚ 1940   📍 NW9 5HJ

 Morden Station
Charles Holden

🕐 1926   📍 SM4 5AZ

1920s London was overcrowded, noisy and dirty. The working class lived in packed grimy slums – mostly in east London – without clean sanitation. But even wealthier residents couldn't escape streets full of horse manure and smog. An alternative was offered with the arrival of electrified railways. Railway operators extended their lines out into the open country surrounding the capital, and built train stations in rolling green fields. Beautifully illustrated print campaigns promoted life in unspoilt nature, just a short commute from the city centre. The suburban dream was born, and tens of thousands of new homes sprung up on the outskirts of London.

Most of the new train stations built in the fields resembled cricket pavilions – simple brick structures with pitched roofs. One such station was the London Underground network's **Colindale Station (006)**, which opened in 1924. It was designed by in-house architect Stanley Heaps, and inoffensively performed its function: offering shelter for passengers and housing a ticket window. Previously, this would have been enough, but managing director of the Underground, Frank Pick, wasn't satisfied – he wanted more from the new stations. He saw these new stations as shop windows for the Underground – modern, rapidly evolving and focused on the future. Pick was one of the first people to grasp the importance of branding and architecture.

Pick hired Manchester-born architect Charles Holden, who was known for his progressive style. Together they changed the face of London and influenced generations of British architects to come. After a couple of trials, Holden's first big job was designing the new Northern Line extension ending at **Morden Station (007)**. This was the world's longest underground railway to date. Eight new stations were designed as a 'set', using the same elements, but adapted for each location. While the ground floor of Morden Station had a wide entrance to allow an uninterrupted flow of people, the first floor opened onto a large window, which featured the massive Underground logo in the centre. The 'roundel', as it is better known, was given unprecedented importance in the designs. With their striking white Portland stone frontages, the stations were hailed as the architecture of a new age.

After the huge success of the Morden extension, Holden's prestige rose, and he was soon tasked with a major commission – the headquarters of the Underground. **55 Broadway (008)** was to become the tallest building in London. The Westminster site on which the building stood was challenging: Underground trains ran just seven metres below ground and the plot was an odd shape. Holden, inspired by his previous work on hospitals, as well as photos of the General Motors Building in Detroit, designed a steel-framed building with a cross-shaped layout. Offices received more daylight and fresh air this way, compared to the traditional office block designs with their central courts.

Dubbed as London's first skyscraper, it also had to deal with strict height restrictions. These limited the height of new buildings to the length of a fireman's ladder – twenty-four metres – to ensure safe evacuation in case of a fire, but also to prevent overshadow in the street. 55 Broadway's top floors were subsequently stepped back (as per the style in New York City) so as not to block any sun, and contained space used only occasionally. This made them passable in the eyes of regulators.

The most prominent sculptors of the day were called on to decorate the building. One of the artists, New York City-born Jacob Epstein, was well known for his controversial work and bohemian lifestyle. His sculptures on the façade shocked the public and were thought to be too vulgar. After several newspapers started a campaign to remove the sculptures, Epstein agreed to shorten a penis on one of the statues.

(008) **55 Broadway**
Charles Holden

🕐 1929 📍 SW1H 0AB ↕ 53M

OXO Tower
Albert Moore

 1928   SE1 9PH   ↕ 67M

Like 55 Broadway, **OXO Tower (009)** also had to overcome building restrictions. Originally a power station from 1900, the building was redesigned by architect Albert Moore into a manufacturing facility for Liebig's Extract of Meat Company, which exported the famous OXO stock cubes around the world. Unfortunately, proposed promotional signs on the roof were not approved, due to advertisement regulations applying to the Thames riverfront.

Moore cunningly overcame the setback by rebuilding the central chimney into an Art Deco tower. On each side, three vertically stacked windows carried the outline of the OXO letters. There's no way to be sure how many stock cubes were sold thanks to this trick, but the tower became a much-loved landmark. When the business closed, the building became neglected and was threatened with demolition.

In a highly unusual move, the Greater London Council bought the building from the owner and then sold it for a fraction of the price to Coin Street Community Builders. This was a group of local residents fighting against the proposed redevelopment of the area into offices. OXO Tower was rebuilt into a successful mixed development with shops, offices and flats. A swanky restaurant with a great view now takes pride of place on the top floor.

Morris T-Type Van

OXO cubes made for the local market were transported in branded company vans. The rest were shipped through the London docks.

Vickers 'Flying Pig' Vulcan

The slow and chubby airliner was produced at Brooklands Aerodrome, just outside of London. The Metropolitan Police, experimenting with airplanes and airships, used the plane in 1923 in an attempt to control notoriously jammed roads during the Epsom Derby.

AEC K-Type Bus

This important design ended the horse-bus influence on the vehicle layout of earlier motor bus models. Passengers on the top deck were unprotected from rain and wind. The buses served until 1932.

 010 **Ideal House**
Raymond Hood

🕐 1929 📍 W1F 7TA

After almost a decade of American-inspired architecture, the master himself, American star architect Raymond Hood, designed a new building in London. **Ideal House (010)** in Soho was essentially a scaled-down version of his American Radiator Building in New York City, built for the same company a couple of years earlier. As with the American original, its façade was clad in black granite: shiny, smooth and flecked with gold.

Despite, or maybe because of, its grandeur, the building received a poor reception from critics on its opening in 1929. The architectural press called it 'alien' and 'in bad taste'. It posed a stark contrast to its neighbour – the half-timbered mock Tudor Liberty Building, which was only four years older. Raymond Hood continued his successful career in the US and went on to become chief architect of the Rockefeller Center in New York City. Ideal House was to remain his only building in Europe.

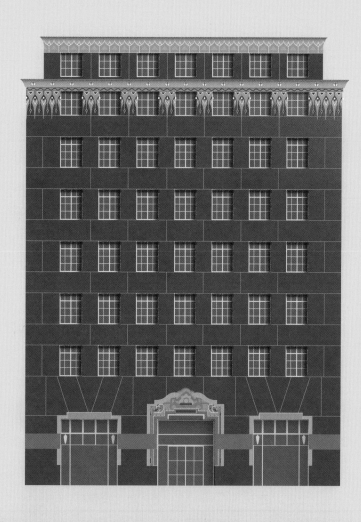

It is 1929 and the Wall Street Crash has triggered global economic collapse. Britain, strongly tied into the global economy and still weakened by the First World War, is taking a direct hit. Factories and businesses are closing, leaving millions without income. In Glasgow, only 50% of people still have a job. But London, again, appears unfazed by the economic slump. While the rest of Britain suffers mass unemployment as many 'old' industries – such as coal mining and shipbuilding – decline, London is becoming a home for all sorts of new businesses. Demand for cars, electrical appliances and other 'London-made' products is rising amid the crisis, ensuring the city's wheels remain firmly in motion.

One of the most popular of these new electrical appliances was the radio, known as the 'wireless' at the time. On its arrival in Britain, a decision was made not to repeat the chaotic expansion of commercial radio stations seen in the US.

A single licence was issued to the British Broadcasting Corporation, which soon expanded and established studios all around town. **Broadcasting House (011)** was designed to put everyone under one roof. The building had to adapt to an odd-shaped site, and what's more, there were height restrictions due to the 'ancient lights' of neighbouring houses.

Ancient 'right to light' legislation protected buildings receiving natural daylight; those that had received unobstructed natural light for more than twenty years could prevent any construction that would block it. This meant that the eastern front had to be redesigned. The building is consequently asymmetrical, sloping on one side with a long mansard roof reaching to the fourth floor. Special attention was given to the construction of soundproof recording studios. They were placed inside a huge brick tower, which was built inside the steel-framed building. More than 2.6 million extra-strong bricks made the walls 1.4 metres thick at the base.

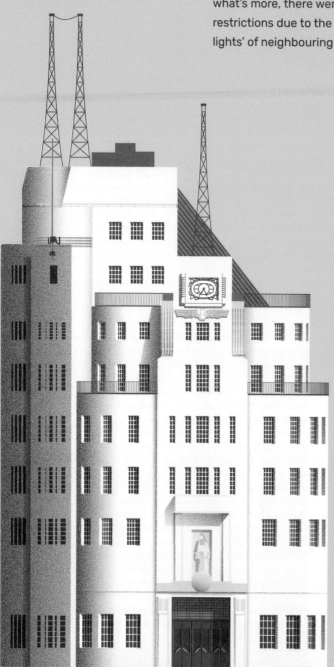

 Broadcasting House
George Val Myer & Raymond McGrath

🕐 1932   📍 W1A 1AA

Morris Royal Air Mail Service Car

This odd-looking car was a one-off, built to promote the newly launched Royal Air Mail Service from Croydon Airport in 1934. The streamlined, aircraft-inspired design turned heads, and the car appeared in commercials and on stamps as far away as New Zealand.

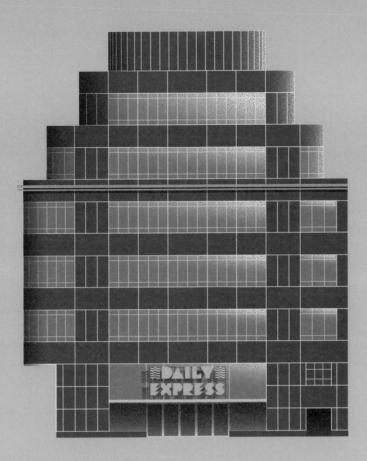

(012) **Daily Express Building**
Ellis and Clarke with
Owen Williams

🕐 1932   📍 EC4A 2BE

Handley Page H.P.42

The huge airliner had luxurious
cabins modelled on the cars
of the Orient Express, which
included a cocktail bar. It was a
remarkably safe but awfully slow
aircraft, with a cruising speed
of only 90mph. It operated from
Croydon Airport, the largest
airport in the UK at the time.

The traditional printed media
were also demonstrating a
progressive architectural style
at the time. The **Daily Express
Building (012)** – on Fleet Street
(where else?) – did its bit in
attracting attention. A streamlined
façade by Ellis and Clark features
rounded corners covered in shiny
black glass. One of the first uses of
curtain façades in Britain made the
surrounding buildings look archaic.

During the construction, a banner
proudly announced: 'Britain's most
modern building for Britain's most
modern newspaper'. It was such
a success that the Daily Express
built its next two branches in
Manchester and Glasgow using
the same black glass façades.

The 1930s saw the golden age of cinemas. The era of silent films was slowly coming to an end, but the **Carlton Cinema (013)** in Islington still opened screenings with a large organ – used to provide both soundtrack and sound effects for silent films. The organ was used frequently, as the cinema staged shows with comedians, dancers and singers between Hollywood blockbusters. Alongside four changing rooms, there were almost 2,300 seats and a café. The exterior is covered in multi-coloured tiles and decorated in Egyptian patterns. It was designed by London-born George Coles, an expert in cinema architecture.

The cinema chain Odeon was established in 1931. Its founder, Oscar Deutsch – from Birmingham – was famous for his extreme working hours and endless energy. In just ten years, he commissioned well over a hundred brand new cinemas around Britain. These new buildings were often the first examples of contemporary architecture ever seen by ordinarily sleepy British towns. Deutsch died prematurely, aged just forty-eight, but still managed to change the look of the British Isles forever. The chain's name comes from ancient Greece and was popular for cinemas in Italy and France, but Deutsch and his publicity team came up with the clever 'Oscar Deutsch Entertains Our Nation'.

Coles became one of Deutsch's favourite architects and helped to develop the 'Odeon Style'. An example of this style is **Woolwich Odeon (014)**, built in 1937. Free of decoration, its streamlined curved façade is covered in glossy cream tiles. The exterior is reminiscent of modernist European architecture, while the interior has a touch of American Art Deco. At night, the whole building would dazzle passers-by with floodlights – a clear bid at detracting attention from the Granada Woolwich, which stood just across the road. The Granada cinema had opened only six months earlier and offered 300 more seats, although its brick façade was definitively less impressive.

(013) **Carlton Cinema**
George Coles

🕐 1930 📍 N1 2TS

FINEST TALKING PICTURES   2500 LUXURY SEATS

FOR THE FIRST TIME
HEAR
HAROLD LLOYD
TALK
in
WELCOME DANGER

 014 **Woolwich Odeon**
George Coles

🕐 1937   📍 SE18 6QJ

Only a month after the Woolwich branch launch, a flagship Odeon cinema opened. The **Leicester Square Odeon (015)** was designed by an ex-fighter pilot from Birmingham called Harry Weedon, alongside Scotsman Andrew Mather. It looked like no other cinema. The façade, made from polished granite, is a striking black. The huge mass of the building is crowned by a thirty-seven-metre-high tower with the Odeon lettering blazing in neon.

It was, and still is, the largest single screen cinema in Britain. The building cost per seat was four times higher than the other major Odeons built at the time. The Leicester Square branch still hosts many major film premieres in Britain, some eighty years later. But most of its contemporaries weren't that lucky. When television invaded British living rooms, cinema audiences sharply declined. Many cinema buildings were closed down or turned into bingo halls. The Carlton in Islington found secondary use as a church.

 015 **Leicester Square Odeon**
Harry Weedon & Andrew Mather

🕐 1937   📍 WC2H 7JY

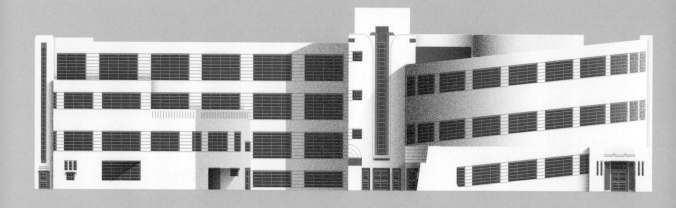

 (016) **Daimler Hire Garage**
Wallis, Gilbert and Partners

🕐 1931 　📍 WC1N 1EX

The automobile industry was another that experienced a huge boost in the 1930s. The driving licence became a legal requirement only in 1934. Before that, anyone over the age of seventeen could drive, with no tests or training needed. As there were very few road rules, more than 1,000 Londoners died on the roads every year, most of them pedestrians and cyclists. The Minister of Transport, Leslie Hore-Belisha, tried to fix that. 'Belisha Beacons' – a black and white pole with a yellow globe on top – were installed at pedestrian crossings around the city and they remain to this day.

A number of well-off Londoners preferred not to own a car, let alone drive one. Instead, they hired limousines with chauffeurs from places such as the **Daimler Hire Garage (016)**. The three-storey building incorporated a huge spiral ramp leading to the top floors, one of the first in the UK to have this feature. Designed by Wallis, Gilbert and Partners, it was opened in 1931. The top floors were used for Daimler cars, while the basement was for privately owned vehicles. The building contained Daimler offices, a petrol station and facilities for chauffeurs. The company was later swallowed by the American Hertz car rental firm. Later, the building served as a garage for taxis and coaches and it is now home to an international advertising agency.

Daimler Double Six

Daimler limousines were a favourite of the European rich and famous. The oldest British car maker even provided official transport for the royal family until 1950.

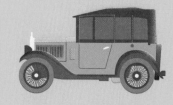

Austin Seven Tourer

At the price of £125, this was one of the first cars that a middle-class British family could afford. People soon nicknamed it a 'bath on wheels' due to its small stature.

de Havilland Express

At the time, this was the fastest British-built passenger aircraft. Operating from Croydon Airport, it was run by the Railway Air Services – an airline oddly operated by four rail companies.

Belisha Beacon

First introduced in 1934, the idea spread as far as New Zealand.

(017) **Victoria Coach Station**
Wallis, Gilbert and Partners

🕐 1932   📍 SW1W 9TP

Wallis, Gilbert and Partners was a partnership between English architect Thomas Wallis and American construction firm Trussed Concrete Steel, which pioneered in reinforced concrete factories in Detroit. Interestingly, it is believed there was in fact no 'Gilbert' at the firm, the name being included simply to make the practice appear larger. After the success of his Firestone Factory (002), Wallis went on to design a number of factories for overseas companies such as Gillette (shaving products), Wrigley's (chewing gum) and Hoover (vacuum cleaners). Wallis' buildings are now regarded as some of the finest examples of 1930s architecture in Britain. But when they opened, the reviews were mostly on the opposite spectrum. It's fair to say that Wallis disliked architecture critics as much as they disliked his buildings. After reading one of the negative reviews, he reportedly visited the editor of *Architectural Review* with a horse whip.

His next building in London, using the same reinforced concrete system, was **Victoria Coach Station (017)**, which is located conveniently near Victoria Train Station. A huge five-storey frontage contained a booking hall, shops, buffet, lounge bar, 200-seat restaurant and offices. On completion in 1932, Wallis, Gilbert and Partners became the first occupants. Behind the building is a station yard, with enough space for seventy-six buses. Much of the traffic of the time was recreational coastal coaches that took Londoners to beaches in Sussex and Kent.

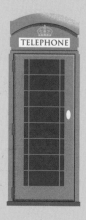

Kiosk No 6

The Telephone Box was designed by Giles Gilbert Scott, the architect of the Battersea Power Station (039). Many remain on London streets to this day, although they are now predominantly used as a background for tourist selfies.

The most famous (and most decorative) building of Wallis, Gilbert and Partners is without a doubt **Hoover Building (018)**. Built for the Ohio-based manufacturer of vacuum cleaners, it was a factory supplying the growing British market. Sitting on Great Western Road alongside a stretch of factories built during this period, it was floodlit at night. The front was faced with snowcrete – a special whitened concrete – and decorated with coloured tiles. The entrance is especially elaborate. Wallis, never bothered with aligning to any existing norms, called his architecture style simply 'fancy'.

Cocky door-to-door salesmen and constant advertising boosted sales and the factory had to expand only two years after opening. During the Second World War, it was repurposed to produce electronic parts for tanks and aircraft. To hide it from German bombers, it was repainted and covered in camouflaged netting. When the factory closed in 1982, Tesco bought the site and turned it into a large supermarket. As of 2018 it remains, although now in the form of snazzy flats.

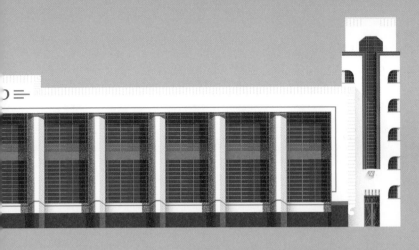

Hoover Building
Wallis, Gilbert and Partners
🕐 1933 📍 UB6 8AT

Air travel was instrumental to London's new global status. Imperial Airways, Britain's largest airline, expanded their operations from Croydon Airport to a flying boat terminal in Southampton. As the number of passengers rose, the company decided to build an **Imperial Airways Terminal (019)** in Victoria. The symmetrical building has a ten-storey clock tower, flanked by five-storey wings. Clad in Portland stone and with a minimalist approach, it looks almost austere from the outside. Amazing Art Deco interiors provided travellers with all the luxury they could desire. In contrast, the back of the building, not visible from the street, was left in brick – probably in an effort to save money. The terminal was built far from any airport, but right by Victoria's Train and Coach Stations. It had direct access to a platform for special first-class trains destined for Southampton.

Imperial Airways Terminal
Albert Lakeman
🕐 1939 📍 SW1W 9SP ↕ 43M

25

(020) **Sudbury Town Station**
Charles Holden

🕐 1931   📍 HA0 2LA

The Underground continued its successful expansion at an even faster pace than before. In just one decade, twenty new stations opened and numerous existing stations were rebuilt. In 1930, the head of the Underground Frank Pick, together with his favourite architect Charles Holden, travelled to the continent to check out the latest architectural trends. They visited Denmark, Germany, the Netherlands and Sweden – admiring in particular the architecture style known as the 'Amsterdam School'. Holden developed a new look for the Underground, which wasn't an imitation of continental architecture, but an adaptation for local materials and use. He called the new stations simply a 'brick box with a concrete lid'. They became an inspiration for a number of new schools, hospitals and power stations around the UK.

The first prototype of the new style for the Underground was **Sudbury Town Station (020)** on the Piccadilly Line. A double-height 'brick box' with large panels of glazing is covered with a 'concrete lid', which overhangs the sides. Unusually, the station's sign on the façade comprised neon tubes that illuminated the station at night. This was the only use of neon in any London station, but it was too expensive to maintain and the sign was taken down in the 1950s.

Chiswick Park Station (021) on the District Line opened a year later. The station sits on an odd corner site, between curving railway tracks and randomly scattered suburban roads. The concept follows the 'brick box with a concrete lid' rule, although the 'box' is drum shaped this time. A sturdy brick tower, whose only purpose is to show off the roundel in the distance, is attached from the west.

(021) **Chiswick Park Station**
Charles Holden

🕐 1932   📍 W4 5NE

022 **Southgate Station**
Charles Holden

🕐 1933 📍 N14 5BH

A1-Class 'Diddler' Trolleybus

At its peak, London had the largest network of trolleybuses in the world. They were much quicker than the trams and buses, and were well liked by passengers.

023 **Page Street Estate**
Edwin Lutyens

🕐 1930 📍 SW1P 4EN

However, the most playful of all the 1930s stations is undoubtedly **Southgate Station (022)**. It's a circular drum with a high central booking hall surrounded by lower offices and shops. The booking hall's ceiling seems to be levitating, supported only by a single pillar in the centre. The cherry on the top is a lighting beacon on the roof, visually inspired by a Tesla coil. Decades later, the beacon became an inspiration for the Daleks in the *Doctor Who* television series.

While the middle class fled to the suburbs with the help of the Underground network, the less wealthy were confined to their old crowded neighbourhoods. The Duke of Westminster donated land to the Westminster City Council for a new social housing project, although under one condition – it had to be designed by Edwin Lutyens, a famous architect known for his palaces in New Delhi and other grand projects. With **Page Street Estate (023)**, Lutyens proved he could operate under a more modest budget. The chequered buildings have one of the earliest examples of gallery access, which helps to increase the floor area of each unit. But what proved most controversial was that every flat had its own toilet. While this was quite common for the middle class, it was not at all usual for working-class tenants. For them, the norm was to use shared outdoor lavatories.

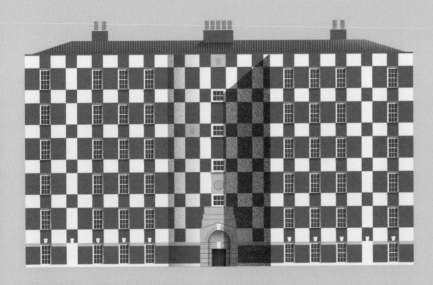

| 024 | **Shell Mex House** |
| | Ernest Joseph |

🕐 1931   📍 WC2R 0HS   ↕ 58M

Somewhat surprisingly in light of the Wall Street Crash, the City saw significant growth during this period. Banks and insurance companies built impressive new offices, and the workforce rose by more than 40% between 1911 and 1938. This placed significant pressure on authorities to review existing building restrictions, and in 1930 a new London Building Act was approved. The maximum height allowance increased from twenty-four metres to thirty metres, but even that wasn't enough. The London County Council started issuing waivers permitting certain buildings to break the limit.

Charming **Shell Mex House (024)** on the Strand, built just a year after the new legislation came in, was way over the new height limit. Its carcass was the Cecil Hotel, which was the largest hotel in Europe with 800 beds. This heavily decorated building was stripped to the bone, reinforced and rebuilt in the Art Deco style. On top of the huge mass of twelve floors sits the largest clock face in the UK. Contemporary Londoners nicknamed it 'Big Benzene'. The clock helped Shell Mex House to beat 55 Broadway (008) in height by five metres.

Cierva C.30

The work of Spanish engineer Juan de la Cierva, the Cierva was a step between an airplane and a helicopter. The Metropolitan Police were very interested in the idea, and trialled the Cierva for surveillance and traffic spotting during the 1930s.

The spectacular **Ibex House (025)** was a speculative development, which offered rental space with all possible services provided. When it opened in 1937, it claimed to be 'the most up-to-date block of City offices'. This was certainly true style-wise, as it embraced a cutting-edge modernism from continental Europe – something unseen in the still very conservative City.

The enormous eleven-storey building is softened with round corners, beige tiles and receding top floors. Its H-plan allows for light to enter every room. Horizontal window bands – the longest strip windows in London – curve around the whole block, reminding one of the work of Erich Mendelsohn, a leading modernist architect who had fled Nazi Germany for Britain a couple of years earlier.

London saw an influx of refugees from Nazi Germany and Central Europe during this period, as tensions on the continent continued to mount. Immigrants included not only Jews, but also influential modern artists and architects whose work the Nazis saw as 'degenerate'. Some of them continued on to the US, while others made Britain their home. Their enriching influence on architecture in both countries is undeniable.

 Ibex House
Fuller, Hall and Foulsham

🕐 1937   📍 EC3N 1DY

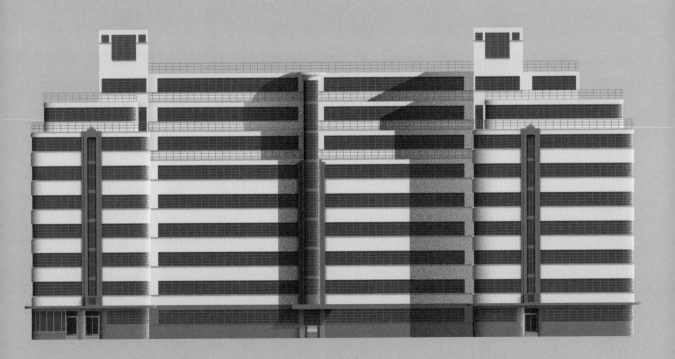

As office space around the capital grew and telephones became more affordable, the number of phone calls increased rapidly. Back then, every call went through a switch station, where operators had to physically connect the right cables for the call to be put through. But a new dial telephone (cutting-edge technology at the time) skipped the human operators and the call was connected by automatic relays.

The **Faraday Building (026)** was built to speed up the calls and to connect London with the outside world. It had 6,000 lines in an automatic exchange and all international telephone calls were routed through it (apart from those to Japan, China and Albania). The façade is neoclassical, but has a great twist – the keystones (the triangular stones crowning the windows and doors) have engraved motifs related to telecommunication, such as telephones and undersea cables.

On completion, the height of the building caused outrage. Although it was nowhere near the tallest building in London, it blocked the view of St Paul's Cathedral from the River Thames. This led to a new law that protected sight-lines to the cathedral and restricted the height of buildings in its vicinity. This law is still in operation, and the Faraday Building remains the tallest between the cathedral and the river (and still obstructs the view).

 Faraday Building
A.R. Myers

🕐 1933   📍 EC4V 4BY   ↕ 47M

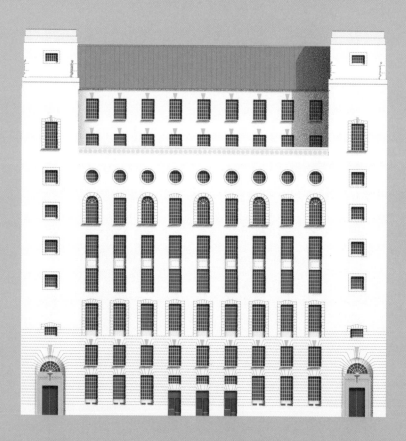

As London's businesses opened their doors to the international market, so too did its education institutions. **Senate House (027)** in Bloomsbury was built by the University of London, the largest university in the world at that time. The university needed to expand and was also determined to improve its prestige globally. Charles Holden was chosen as the architect, partly because of his experience with 55 Broadway (008). The brief asked for a building that would stand the test of time and that wouldn't go out of fashion once tastes changed.

When completed in 1937, Senate House became the tallest building in London, beating Shell Mex House (024) by six metres. The university's vice chancellor fittingly described it as 'something that could not have been built by any earlier generation than this, and can only be at home in London'. As with any new architecture, it wasn't to everyone's taste. The tower's huge undecorated mass was intended to show the university as a permanent institution, but Londoners had other ideas. With war looming once again, people connected its style with strict Nazi architecture, and a rumour spread that Hitler desired it as his British headquarters.

However, as if to prove the rumour false, the Luftwaffe bombed the building during the Blitz. During the Second World War, the Ministry of Information moved in. Contrary to its name, the ministry's main tasks were censorship, propaganda and manipulation of facts. Both the building and the institution inspired George Orwell's all-controlling 'Ministry of Truth' in his anti-utopian novel *1984*. Little surprise then that the building appeared in the film adaptation as well.

Austin 'High Lot' Taxicab

The first taxi designed especially for London. It earned its nickname due to the unusually high roof, which allowed passengers to keep their top hats on.

(027) **Senate House**
Charles Holden

🕐 1937   📍 WC1E 7HU   ↕ 64M

Britain is once again at war and London is getting ready. Tens of thousands of children are being evacuated to the countryside, while the streets are crowding with soldiers. The government has taken over numerous buildings in the capital and factories are being ordered to change production to help arm the troops. In city parks, vegetable patches appear as Britain does its best to become self-sufficient in food production. Fearing Luftwaffe bombers, strategic buildings are being camouflaged and many have anti-aircraft guns installed on their roofs. Strict black-out rules hide London from bombers at night. Street lights go off, every house puts up thick, dark curtains and vehicles have their headlights obscured. Only thin strips of light shine through.

40

DAILY WORKER

UNDERGROUND

UNDERGROUND

UNDERGROUND

PENIVALE STATION

PENIVALE STATION

WEST ACTON STATION

CENTRAL LINE

CENTRAL LINE

028
Waltham Forest Town Hall
Philip Dalton Hepworth
🕐 1942   📍 E17 4JF

A shortage of material and labour during the Second World War meant that many plans for new buildings in the 1940s were postponed until after the war. Any construction already under way was delayed and finished with revised plans. This was exactly the case for **Waltham Forest Town Hall (028)**. Hampstead-born Philip Dalton Hepworth won the competition for its design. Construction began in 1937, but when war broke out it was still only a shell. The building was eventually completed in 1942. The design of the façade is an austere style of Scandinavian modern architecture. Unfortunately, the interior had to be simplified and the materials replaced with cheaper alternatives. Plywood and terrazzo took the place of oak and marble, and sculptures for the entrance were never made.

The expansion of the Underground also had to be shelved. One of the few buildings to be completed relatively on schedule was **West Acton Station (029)**. Its construction was already under way before the war and it opened in 1940. The small station is a concrete box, clad in brick, with full-height windows separated with concrete bars. It was the first station designed by Tasmanian Brian Lewis – his other designs had to wait until after the war to be realised.

Fordson 7V Fire Engine

Fighting the fires ignited by bombs was the National Fire Service, made up of both men and women. The red fire trucks were painted grey, so as not to attract the attention of the Luftwaffe.

029
West Acton Station
Brian Lewis
🕐 1940   📍 W3 0LG

Surprisingly, a year into the war, central London still hadn't been bombed. When the Battle of Britain commenced, the Luftwaffe focused mostly on Royal Air Force airfields and airplane factories. London was strictly off-limits for German bombers. As a result, many evacuated children returned to the city. But at the end of August 1940, the Germans accidentally bombed Oxford Street and the West End. Winston Churchill ordered a swift reprisal and in just twenty-four hours the RAF had bombed Berlin. British bombs didn't cause as much damage on the ground as they did to Hitler's ego. Days later, he promised to raze British cities to the ground. The Blitz on Britain began in earnest.

Hawker Hurricane

Although less photogenic than the Spitfire, sturdy Hurricanes accounted for 60% of victories in the Battle of Britain. This airplane was based at Croydon Airport, protecting London from bombers.

Day after day, night after night, hundreds of bombers terrorised the city. The East End was severely damaged, because of its proximity to the docks and warehouses, but other parts were not spared either. People built their own air raid shelters in their gardens and Underground stations were turned into shelters overnight. Ironically, this shift of the Luftwaffe's focus from RAF airfields towards British cities gave the weakened Royal Air Force breathing space to re-arm. Intense bombing of London continued until May 1941, when the Germans – with a bloodied nose – turned their attentions towards the Soviet Union.

V1 'Doodlebug' Flying Bomb

These pilot-less flying bombs terrorised Londoners in 1944. Almost 10,000 were launched from the French and Dutch coasts – luckily the autopilot wasn't very precise.

Dornier Do 17

The German bomber was nicknamed the 'flying pencil' for its slim fuselage. This airplane was rammed by an RAF fighter during an air raid in 1940 and crashed into Victoria Train Station, incredibly causing no casualties on the ground. Caught on camera, the event became a sensation and Ray Holmes, the pilot, a hero.

In 1944, when most Londoners considered the war practically over, a new threat came from the sky. V1 flying bombs hit the streets. The British public nicknamed them 'doodlebugs' for their buzzing sound. Most of them were landing short, meaning south London took the toll. But the worst was yet to come. The increasingly desperate Nazis had one last secret weapon, for which there was no defence. It was faster than the speed of sound, built by slave labour in underground caves and designed by Wernher von Braun, who later got the Americans onto the moon. The V2 rocket. It hit London so fast that people had no idea what had happened. The government, keen on keeping the public calm, claimed that explosions were from leaking gas at first. Lives and homes continued to be lost.

030 AIROH
🕐 1945

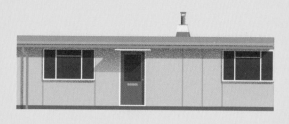

031 UNI-SECO
🕐 1945

On 8 May 1945, the war in Europe finally ended. A five-year nightmare was over and people celebrated in the streets. But the grim reality lingered. In London, tens of thousands had lost their lives and more than a million buildings had been destroyed or damaged. There were hundreds of thousands of homeless families. A third of East End homes had been wiped out. And on top of all this, servicemen were returning from the battlefields. The housing crisis was at its most acute.

Churchill and the government decided on prefabricated houses as a quick fix. Factories previously producing arms now turned their attention to making new homes. **AIROH (030)** prefabs were jointly produced in aircraft factories such as AW Hawksley and the Bristol Aeroplane Co. They were built completely from aluminium and produced at incredible speed – one house every twelve minutes. The prefab was made up of four fully furnished parts, which were connected together by a crane on site.

UNI-SECO (031) prefabs, produced in London, had a timber frame and asbestos walls. Thousands of these homes were built across London by German and Italian prisoners of war (many of whom were held in Britain until 1948). Designed to last only ten years, most of them were destroyed when residents moved into new estates in the 1950s and 1960s. Incredibly, part of the UNI-SECO Excalibur Estate in Catford, south London, still survives.

AEC RT Gas-Powered Bus

To save precious fuel, some London buses were converted to run on gas, which was produced by a small and smelly trailer towed behind. The buses were slow and generally ran on routes without hills.

Hanger Lane Station
Brian Lewis

🕐 1949   📍 W5 1DL

Continual bombing had also badly damaged London's transport system. Infrastructure needed reconstruction and rolling stock was in a bad state. Plans from before the war came to fruition very slowly. **Hanger Lane Station (032)** was designed by Brian Lewis in 1938, but it was completed more than ten years later. The station's circular plan is a nod to Southgate – sadly, it lost many of the original details and can't really compare with the pre-war stations.

One stop away is **Perivale Station (033)**, another pre-war design by Lewis. It was much simplified and built without a planned wing and tower, but its concave red brick façade with large glazed section is still elegant and interesting. By the time the stations opened, Lewis had already left Britain. He later became an important architect in post-war Australia.

Perivale Station
Brian Lewis

🕐 1947   📍 UB6 8AE

V-2 Rocket

The rockets were faster than sound and hit the streets quite literally out of the blue. When the government tried to conceal the attacks as gas explosions, some started calling them 'flying gas pipes'.

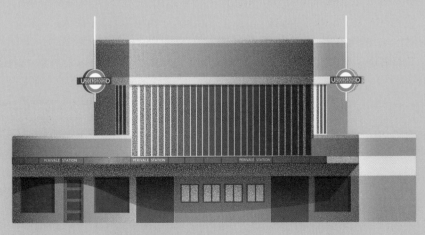

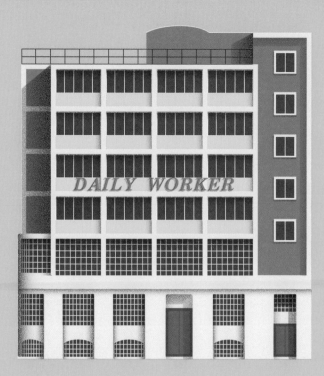

 William Rust House
Ernő Goldfinger

🕐 1946　📐 1988　📍 EC1M 3PS

Although victorious, Britain was on its knees. The cost of war, especially that of the American weapons, drained the country's finances and gold reserves. Practically bankrupt, it had to secure a massive loan from the US, which ended up taking sixty-one years to pay off. The new Labour government, elected after the war, greatly improved the lives of many by founding the National Health Service and providing free healthcare, but the economy struggled to recover. The rationing of food and other products lasted well into the 1950s.

Grim living conditions led to increased support for the British Communist Party. The *Daily Worker* was the party's newspaper, but its offices were burned down in the Blitz. A bomb-damaged brush-and-sponge warehouse was bought in 1945 and Hungarian architect Ernő Goldfinger was hired to refashion it into what became known as **William Rust House (034)**. Goldfinger, who became notorious for his brutalist tower blocks some twenty years later, was glad for any commission. Construction took three long years and some of the work was done by volunteers over the weekends. The modest façade of the *Daily Worker* offices seems tame in comparison to Goldfinger's later work. The building was taken down in 1988 and replaced by a generic office building.

When the Olympics came to London in 1948, the cash-strapped government couldn't afford to invest in new sports facilities. Existing grounds were used and the main venue was the Empire Stadium (now Wembley); it was converted from a greyhound track just two weeks before the opening ceremony. Olympic Way, the grand road access to the stadium, was built by German prisoners of war, although Germany was not invited to compete in the games. The Olympic Village, which usually accommodates the competitors, wasn't built at all, so the athletes had to sleep in army camps and college gyms. Athletes even had to bring their own towels.

Short Solent

Short Brothers transformed its military design into a passenger flying boat. It was shown off in London on the River Thames and then operated a link between Southampton and Johannesburg.

(035) **Spa Green Estate, Tunbridge House**
Berthold Lubetkin

🕐 1949   📍 EC1V 4PP

With this austerity as a backdrop, **Spa Green Estate (035)** in Clerkenwell seemed like something from another planet. This was model social housing with a generous budget. It set the bar so high that most of the other estates of the era didn't come close by comparison, especially when funds dried out. It was designed by Georgia-born architect Berthold Lubetkin, who had built luxury housing blocks in the 1930s, and also the Finsbury Health Centre, a pioneering attempt to provide free healthcare to the masses. The three blocks that comprise Spa Green are set apart, so as not to cast shadows on each other.

Clever structural engineering by Ove Arup gave Lubetkin an almost free hand for façade design. He created abstract compositions, similar to textiles he had studied and admired. Bricks and tiles are supported with bold colours, referencing Russian constructivism. Residents who were lucky enough to live there had to follow a set of strict rules: they were forbidden to hang washing on balconies as it would spoil the architecture; no rubbish could be emptied after 11am; stairs had to be swept every day and washed every week on a rota basis; and at 8pm, a whistle sounded and all the children had to leave the playground and go home.

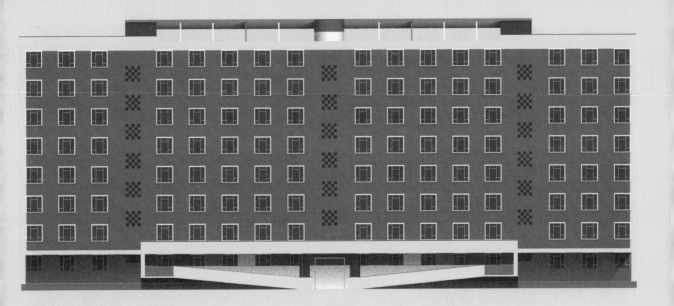

ROYAL FESTIVAL HALL

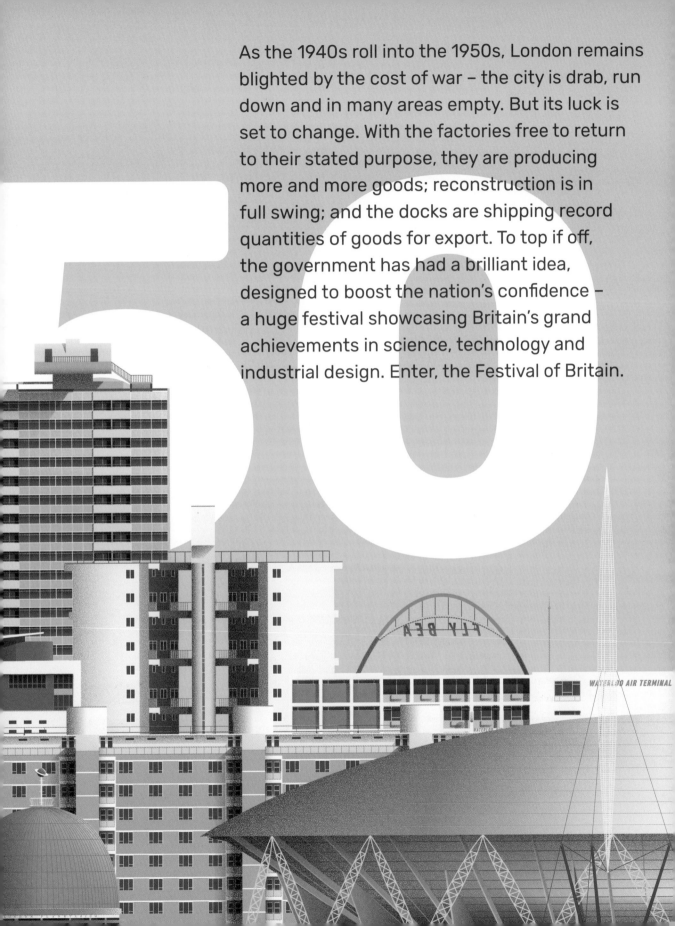

As the 1940s roll into the 1950s, London remains blighted by the cost of war – the city is drab, run down and in many areas empty. But its luck is set to change. With the factories free to return to their stated purpose, they are producing more and more goods; reconstruction is in full swing; and the docks are shipping record quantities of goods for export. To top if off, the government has had a brilliant idea, designed to boost the nation's confidence – a huge festival showcasing Britain's grand achievements in science, technology and industrial design. Enter, the Festival of Britain.

WATERLOO AIR TERMINAL

FLY BEA

The South Bank – a derelict industrial zone - was chosen as the main site for the extravaganza named the Festival of Britain. Most of the architects and designers behind the festival were very young, in their twenties and thirties. Their bold and progressive visions were realised in the festival's twenty-seven pavilions. The fair was a revolution not only in design, but also in materials and technology. A mix of aluminium, plastic, concrete and glass shaped the buildings and influenced British architecture for years to come. The planning of the festival started in 1947 and the event ran from May to September 1951. The primary audience was the UK itself, however the event was advertised in thirty-four different countries abroad. London Transport sent four double-decker buses with built-in exhibitions on a tour around Europe to attract potential visitors.

The **Royal Festival Hall (036)** was built as the centrepiece of the festival and is the only surviving festival structure on the South Bank. Constructed from the best available materials, it was also a replacement for London's greatest concert auditorium, Queen's Hall, which was lost in the Blitz. Noise and vibrations from a nearby railway bridge were dealt with using an innovative approach known as the 'egg in a box'. The auditorium is suspended in the centre of the building and the surrounding space cancels out the unwanted noise. During construction, the site was visited by modernist legends such as Le Corbusier, Walter Gropius, Marcel Breuer and Frank Lloyd Wright, who had nothing but praise for it.

English architect Ralph Tubbs, who was Ernő Goldfinger's unpaid intern before the war, was only in his thirties when he designed the **Dome of Discovery (037)**. The festival's largest and most futuristic building had a sleek silhouette, reminiscent of a flying saucer. It was the largest aluminium structure in the world and a symbol of the optimism of Tubbs' generation. Inside was a huge scientific exhibition, showcasing the feats of British innovation, including radar, jet engines, nuclear power stations and penicillin. What's more, you could send a signal to the moon via a satellite dish installed on top of a 'Shot tower' on site.

(036) **Royal Festival Hall**
Robert Matthew,
Leslie Martin,
Pete Moro

🕐 1951   📍 SE1 8XX

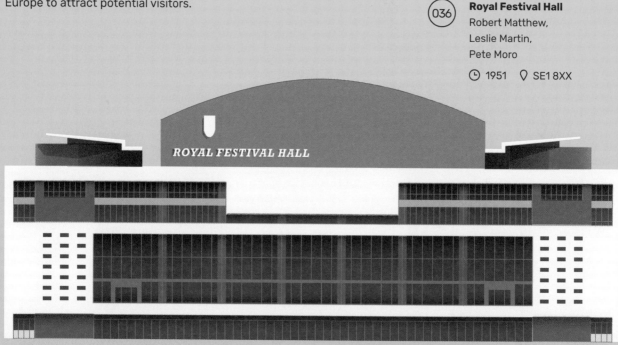

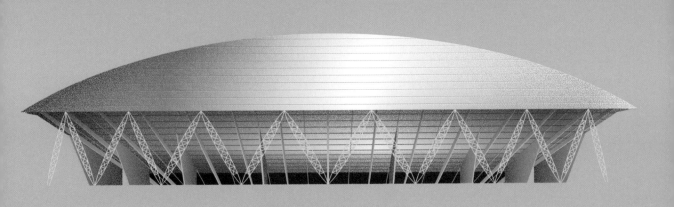

 Dome of Discovery
Ralph Tubbs

🕐 1951 🏗 1952 📍 SE1 9PX

A competition for a structure that would attract attention from north of the river was won by American-born Hidalgo Moya and Englishman Philip Powell, both in their twenties. They teamed up with Austrian structural engineer Felix Samuely to build a gravity-defying steel structure called **Skylon (038)**. Shaped like a cigar and supported only by thin steel cables, the (seemingly) levitating structure was just a couple of metres shorter than Big Ben. Visitors joked that Skylon was similar to the British economy – it had no visible means of support. The Dome of Discovery and Skylon inspired Richard Rogers when designing the Millennium Dome (100) at Greenwich Peninsula half a century later.

After just four months, the gates of the festival site closed. The Festival of Britain was a huge success – 8.5 million visitors came. It changed British architecture, art and crafts for decades to come. It was also a place of fun and education for the working and middle classes from all over. But people on the political right saw this through a very different prism. Churchill hated the idea and called it 'three-dimensional Socialist propaganda'. Sure enough, when he won the general election that autumn, his first act as a prime minister was to order the clearing of the site. Most of the pavilions were only temporary anyway, but even the popular Dome of Discovery and Skylon were sold for scrap metal.

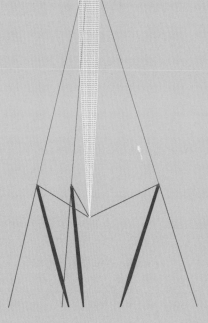

 Skylon
Hidalgo Moya, Philip Powell
& Felix Samuely

🕐 1951 🏗 1952 📍 SE1 9PX

Indeed, streets were changing fast. The system of electric tramways was thought to be too inflexible and outdated. Instead of investing in their improvement, it proved cheaper to replace them with new diesel buses. On 2 July 1952, the last tram retired to its depot. Even with the trams out of the picture, electricity consumption rose, and numerous coal-fired power stations filled the air with smoke. The coal fired in the power stations and in homes was low grade, because most of the better quality coal was exported abroad, to supply much needed cash.

That winter, the smoke, combined with diesel emissions and thick fog (due to an absence of wind), caused chaos in the streets. Visibility was so bad that even cinemas had to close because people couldn't see the screen. All public transport apart from the Underground network came to a halt, as did the ambulance service. The Great Smog lasted less than a week but it resulted in as many as 12,000 deaths in London, largely from bronchitis and pneumonia.

One of the buildings blamed for the Great Smog was **Battersea Power Station (039)**. Although it started producing electricity in 1933, its fourth and last chimney was finished some twenty years later. Its brickwork was designed by English architect and designer Giles Gilbert Scott, who was known for combining gothic and modern architecture. The multi-disciplinary designer was also responsible for Liverpool Cathedral and the iconic red telephone box.

The power station was, at the time, the largest brick building in the world. An experimental system was used to reduce sulphur emissions. It effectively 'washed' the smoke, but the truth is it worsened the situation. The by-product released into the River Thames was extremely toxic and the practice had to be stopped in the 1960s. The station ceased to operate in 1983, and after decades of decay is now being redeveloped into luxury flats, offices and shopping spaces.

 Battersea Power Station
Giles Gilbert Scott

🕐 1955 📍 SW8 5BN

Waterloo Air Terminal
John Burnet, Tait and Partners
🕐 1953   🗓 1957   ♀ SE1 7NJ

Festival Star

The Festival of Britain logo was created by Abram Games, one of the greatest British graphic designers of the twentieth century. It appeared on everything from printed materials to vehicles and buildings.

The 1950s saw air travel become a habit for well-heeled Londoners. London (later Heathrow) Airport didn't have the best transport links yet and so the **Waterloo Air Terminal (040)** was used as a check-in facility. The terminal was inside the modified Station Gate building, still standing after the Festival of Britain, where it had served as an entrance to the festival area and Underground station below. Impressive laminated arches were made from timber donated by the Canadian Lumbermen's Association.

The repurposed building was used by British European Airways and other European airlines between 1953 and 1957. A heliport behind the building saw some lucky passengers using helicopters as the fastest way to the airport, but most of them travelled on a fleet of buses.

Westland Whirlwind

The helicopter service between the terminal at South Bank and London Airport ran seven times a day. Many people used the seventeen-minute journey as a sightseeing flight. Floats were added in case of an emergency landing on the River Thames.

Hallfield Estate
Denys Lasdun,
Berthold Lubetkin,
Lindsay Drake

🕐 1958 📍 W2 6EL

AEC Regal IV 4RF4

British European Airways owned a fleet of sixty-five custom-built coaches. These one-and-a-half deckers had increased luggage capacity. They were replaced in the 1960s by the Routemaster buses, which towed luggage trolleys.

New housing was a top priority for local councils during this period. One large area in Bayswater, which was previously occupied by rows of terraced houses and made vacant by bombs and a V1, became **Hallfield Estate (041)**. A competition for the design was won by Tecton, led by Berthold Lubetkin. But before the construction started, the practice fell apart. Lubetkin, disillusioned after clashing with authorities on other projects, retreated to his isolated farm in Gloucestershire, where he took up farming. He still practised architecture, although in limited form.

The estate was eventually realised by two former members of Tecton — Denys Lasdun and Lindsay Drake. The original plan, devised right after the war when the housing crisis was at its most acute, had called for high density. But the plan was revisited and the density lowered by the removal of the top floors, and two of the blocks entirely. The remaining fifteen blocks now range between ten and six storeys high. The pleasing pattern on the building's façade is comprised of balconies, which also provide access to the flats.

AEC RT 'Bridge Jumper' Bus

In 1952, the number 78 bus was crossing Tower Bridge when the bridge started to open. The quick-thinking driver accelerated and the bus flew over the enlarging gap. Passengers suffered only minor injuries.

Completely different from most of the emerging housing projects was **Sulkin House (042)**. Denys Lasdun was helping to realise Hallfield Estate, but he was also meeting residents of crowded terraces in east London to find out what they liked about them. Rather than being repaired, streets of Victorian terraces were razed to make space for new development. Lasdun designed an eight-storey building containing twenty-four maisonettes.

It is split into two residential blocks, connected by a separate core containing the stairwell and refuse chutes. This isolates the noise and allows more air and light into the building. Units face each other, to encourage neighbourly interaction. Lasdun, perhaps naively, hoped this would help recreate the life and relationships of the former East End streets. The architect built two more 'cluster' towers — Trevelyan House and Keeling House.

 (042) **Sulkin House**
Denys Lasdun

🕐 1958 📍 E2 6PG

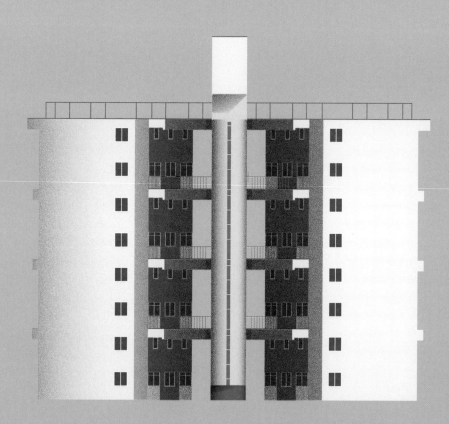

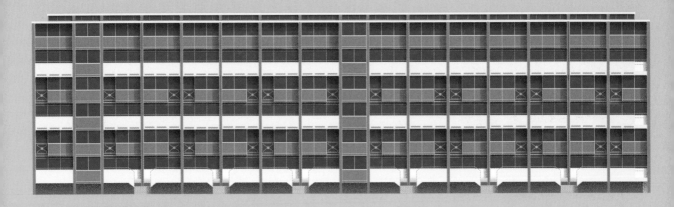

 Golden Lane Estate
Chamberlin, Powell and Bon

🕐 1956   📍 EC1Y 0TN

Having suffered severe damage by fire bombs during the war, the City was an area of London in particular need of attention. In 1950, only 500 people still lived in the area. In an effort to boost residential numbers, local authorities organised a competition to design a new estate. Three teachers at Kingston Polytechnic – Indian-born Geoffry Powell, Londoner Peter Chamberlin and Swiss Christoph Bon – sent individual proposals, but agreed that if one of them won, they would form a studio together.

Powell (no relation to Skylon's Philip Powell) won the competition and the famous practice of Chamberlin, Powell and Bon was born. **Golden Lane Estate (043)** was a council estate, built to house essential City workers at subsidised rents. Most of the flats were designed for singles and couples, as families were not a top priority here. The residents enjoyed great facilities, including a swimming pool, badminton courts, a bowling green, a nursery, a playground and workshops. Unusually for the time, the whole area was pedestrianised, with no access for cars.

Golden Lane Estate was crowned by **Great Arthur House (044)**. Fifty metres tall, with seventeen floors, it became the highest residential building in London. Its optimistic yellow façade teams up with the red and blue of the lower blocks. On the roof is a curvy concrete quiff, hiding inside it a lift and water machinery. Inspired by Le Corbusier's Unité d'Habitation, the three-level roof also had a pool, pergola and trees. However, following a suicide and vandalism, the roof has sadly been locked away.

Morris J-Type Van

Replaced the last horse-drawn carts in London. It was a very popular delivery van in the 1950s, seen in the livery of the Royal Mail. The surviving cars now often serve as fashionable food trucks.

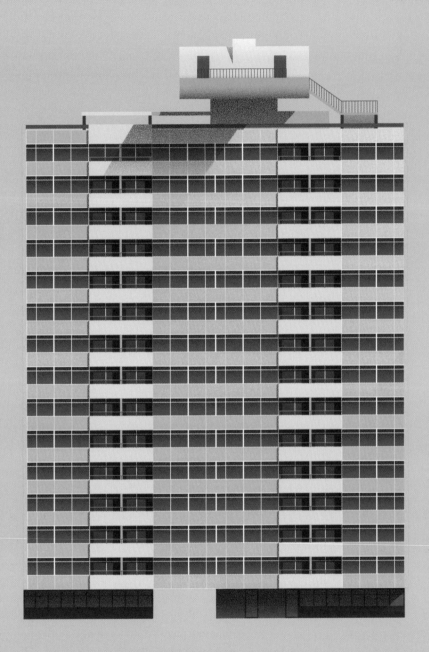

 Great Arthur House
Chamberlin, Powell and Bon

🕐 1957   📍 EC1Y 0RE

Some contemporary architects saw British post-war architecture as too 'soft', believing that it diluted the idea of modernism. Perhaps the best place to see the difference between both camps is Alton Estate in Roehampton. The earlier eastern side is mostly Scandinavian-inspired – a 'soft' combination of low-rise buildings and towers, designed by an architecture team led by Rosemary Stjernstedt from Birmingham, who spent six years working as a town planner in Sweden. But the west side of the estate is dramatically different.

Five ultra-modern 'slab' blocks on **The Highcliffe Drive (045)** were designed by young progressive architects, and the influence of their visit to the recently finished Unité d'Habitation by Le Corbusier is clearly evident. Built on pilotis, it seems like the massive blocks are floating over the grassy slope. Inside, spacious two-floor maisonettes span the width of the building, allowing for windows on both the northern and southern sides. The buildings appeared in François Truffaut's 1966 film adaptation of the dystopian novel *Fahrenheit 451*.

The construction of these buildings coincided with an optimistic plan for rebuilding post-war London. Named after its author Patrick Abercrombie, the Abercrombie Plan was an attempt to change the whole fabric of London for the better. It proposed many changes, but the primary aim was to make London smaller and cleaner, and to move a portion of the population and some industry to New Towns built in the countryside. The reality proved more difficult and only fractions of the plan were realised.

 The Highcliffe Drive
LCC Architects' Department
led by Colin Lucas

🕐 1958   📍 SW15 4PX

(046) **Churchill Gardens Estate**
Powell and Moya
Architect Practice

🕐 1951   📍 SW1V 3HU

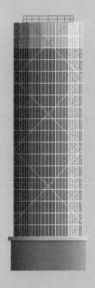

Accumulator tower at Churchill Gardens Estate

The only estate built according to the Abercrombie Plan was **Churchill Gardens Estate (046)**. Westminster Council selected a proposal by Philip Powell and Hidalgo Moya, who were only in their mid-twenties. The large estate was built from 1946 to 1962 and replaced an area of Victorian terraces badly damaged during the Blitz. Uniquely, the estate had a district heating system – the first of its kind in Britain. A clever system collected surplus heat from Battersea Power Station via a tunnel under the River Thames.

A glazed accumulator tower, also designed by Powell and Moya, distributed heat around the estate. The site contains thirty-two blocks ranging from three to eleven storeys high, and housing some 5,000 residents. Efforts to accommodate a balanced cross-section of society were largely successful. Residents of the elite (and expensive) Dolphin Square soon complained about their flats not being as nice as the ones on the council estate across the road.

(047) **Congress House**
David du Roi Aberdeen

🕐 1958 📍 WC1B 3LS

The post-war decade also saw a change in the demands and rights of London's workers. New power gained by trade unions materialised in the construction of **Congress House (047)**. It opened in 1958, ten years after English architect David du Roi Aberdeen won the competition. The façade is clad in grey polished granite. Unusually, the main assembly hall is in the basement and receives natural light through an inner courtyard, which serves as a light well.

Sitting over the glass ceiling is a sculpture by Jacob Epstein, carved on the spot from a single ten-ton stone. Most of the ground floor is open, broken only by columns. Impressive curved glass, covering the circular staircase leading to the basement, breaks the grid system. The building was a reflection of the strength of the trade unions during this period. Over the next few decades, their influence diminished.

LCC E/1 Tramway

These tram cars were introduced in London in 1910 and served for an incredible forty-two years. The last week of their service in 1952 saw emotional goodbyes and overcrowded cars as people scrambled for one last ride.

AEC Routemaster

Without a doubt the most famous of all London buses. It was operated by a driver and a conductor, who stood on the open boarding platform at the back. The (relatively) reliable buses served on London streets for an unbelievable forty-nine years.

Austin FX4

The iconic taxi was launched in 1958 and stayed in production for an incredible forty years until 1998. This was largely because there wasn't enough money to develop a new design to replace it.

During the 1950s, tensions between the West and the Soviet Union culminated in Cold War. Britain's role as a global super power was superseded by that of the Soviet Union and the US, and the two became determined to prove the other less advanced. On 4 October 1957, a small metal ball named Sputnik left Earth and circulated the globe while emitting a beeping sound. Radio amateurs from around the world tuned in. The Americans were shocked, and soon committed their best brains and huge sums of money to outstripping the Soviets. The space race was on. Meanwhile, Britain opted for a more down-to-earth approach – in 1958 the **London Planetarium (048)** opened on Baker Street.

It was the first planetarium in the Commonwealth, and unlike most at the time, it was a commercial gig rather than a government-backed university project. As the only planetarium in London, it drew in huge crowds, including many London schoolchildren. But in 2006, after years of declining visitor numbers, the planetarium ceased astronomical projections. Renamed the Stardome, visitors were instead treated to a 360-degree cartoon film about celebrity (the result of a business partnership with Madame Tussauds). *The Wonderful World of Stars* received a cold reception from astronomy fans. Luckily, the Peter Harrison Planetarium opened at the National Maritime Museum in Greenwich only a year later.

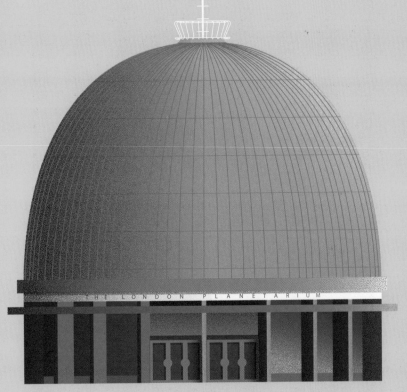

 London Planetarium
G. Watt

🕐 1958   📍 NW1 5LR

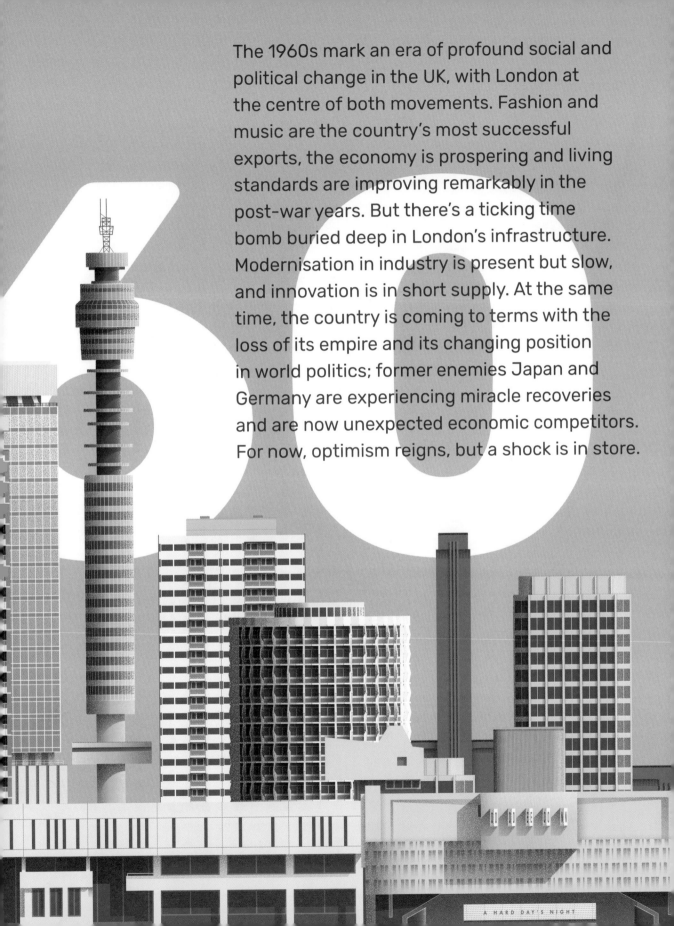

The 1960s mark an era of profound social and political change in the UK, with London at the centre of both movements. Fashion and music are the country's most successful exports, the economy is prospering and living standards are improving remarkably in the post-war years. But there's a ticking time bomb buried deep in London's infrastructure. Modernisation in industry is present but slow, and innovation is in short supply. At the same time, the country is coming to terms with the loss of its empire and its changing position in world politics; former enemies Japan and Germany are experiencing miracle recoveries and are now unexpected economic competitors. For now, optimism reigns, but a shock is in store.

As the pavilions of the 1951 Festival of Britain were demolished, part of the South Bank site was taken over by the Royal Dutch Shell Group, a massive British-Dutch oil corporation. The **Shell Centre (049)**, its new UK headquaters, opened ten years after the festival closed its gates. While the festival architecture had been progressive and futuristic, the Shell Centre looked to the past. Dull, monotone façades were clad in Portland stone and the windows were framed in bronze. Surprisingly so, since the architect – Salt Lake City-born Howard Robertson – had helped design the strikingly modernist UN headquarters in New York City.

Two large nine-storey blocks accompanied a 107-metre-tall tower, which was the tallest office building in London at the time. The complex as a whole became the largest office building in Europe, by floor space. Staff enjoyed lavish facilities such as squash courts, a swimming pool, badminton courts, a cinema, restaurants, a theatre, exhibition spaces and even a rifle range. The complex is now being redeveloped and the tower, the only surviving part of the original development, now heads a whole cluster of high-rises.

Shell Centre
Howard Robertson

🕑 1961   📍 SE1 7NA   ↕ 107M

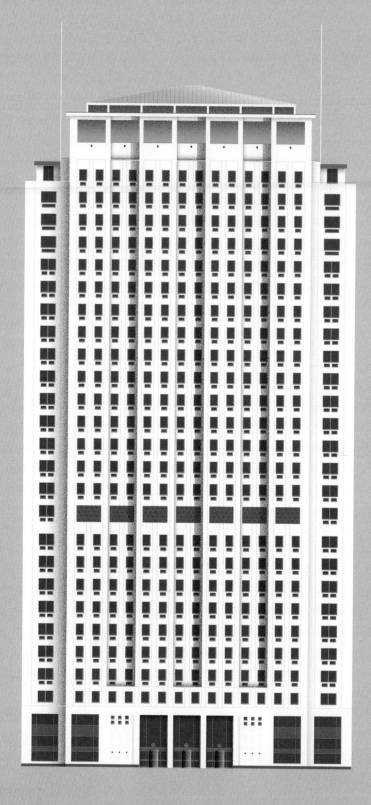

If the Shell Centre was old fashioned, **Vickers Tower (050)** (now renamed Millbank Tower) was cutting edge. Designed by Ronald Ward and Partners, it opened just two years later, and was pioneering in its glass curtain façade – a lightweight structure that acts as the building's 'skin'. It beat the Shell Centre in height by eleven metres, and the curved tower resembles a butterfly in plan. As its name suggests, it was originally built for Vickers, a famous engineering company that produced military and civil aeroplanes, tanks and trucks. This was a high point for the company – it would later be subsumed by various mergers, a result of the gradual nationalisation of the whole industry that occurred over subsequent decades.

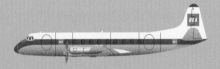

Vickers Viscount

The first turboprop airliner in the world became the most successful product of post-war British civil aviation.

 Vickers Tower
Ronald Ward and Partners

🕐 1963   📍 SW1P 4QP   ↕ 118M

The renewal of the City that had begun in the previous decade continued in earnest during this period. Tottenham-born architect William H. Rogers was one of the key figures in the regeneration project, and his innovative office buildings replaced many of the burned-out shells left after the war – in many cases merging different sites together to allow for even greater buildings. Rogers travelled to New York and Chicago, where he admired towering skyscrapers clad in curtain wall façades. Back in London, he had to battle with conservative City planners for every floor.

His **20 Fenchurch Street (051)** was the 'first generation' skyscraper in the City. A central core was topped with a huge three-storey-high roof structure. This massive 'umbrella' carried the curtain façade that covered the entire building. The feat of engineering ensured the interior was free of clutter – something unseen at the time, when thick structural walls or series of columns fractured standard office spaces. The windows of the sleek, lightweight façade were covered in a reflective film in order to protect the space from overheating in the sun.

20 Fenchurch Street
William H. Rogers

🕐 1968   📍 EC3M 8AF   ↕ 91M

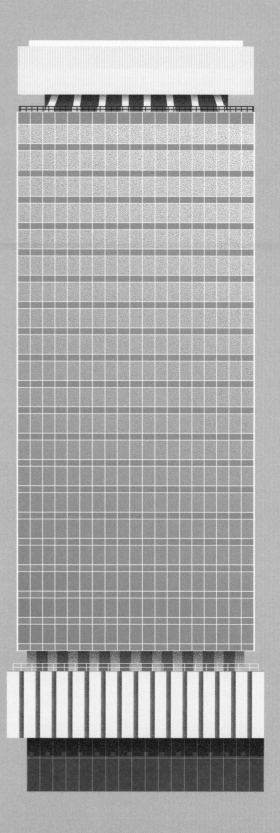

Although the building was pragmatic in design, the continuous improvement of construction technology and rising office standards made it obsolete. In the never-ending cycle of the redevelopment of central London, the building had to make way for a new generation. Its unusual top-hung structure was a headache for demolition experts in 2008. Six years later, it was replaced by the Walkie Talkie (116) – a skyscraper almost twice as high as the previous building.

While most of London's commercial architecture experiences a relatively short life span, traditional institutions have always been keen to build landmarks designed to stand the test of time. **The Royal College of Physicians (052)** wanted to rebrand itself as modern and accessible. Its new building was an ideal opportunity to do just that. Denys Lasdun was selected as the architect because of his uncompromisingly modern and confident work. But the architect wasn't thinking only about looks; he was focused on the function and the people inside.

Lasdun spent weeks observing aspects of RCP life in the old building. Its new home next to Regent's Park was designed with this research in mind. The three-storey building sees each floor grow larger, resulting in an inverted ziggurat shape – not an uncommon feature in modernist design. Narrow vertical windows, designed to avoid the potential distraction of a good view, are seemingly randomly scattered around. The building is now listed, and highly rated to this day – something that sets it apart from its contemporaries.

 (052) **The Royal College of Physicians**
Denys Lasdun

🕐 1964   📍 NW1 4LE

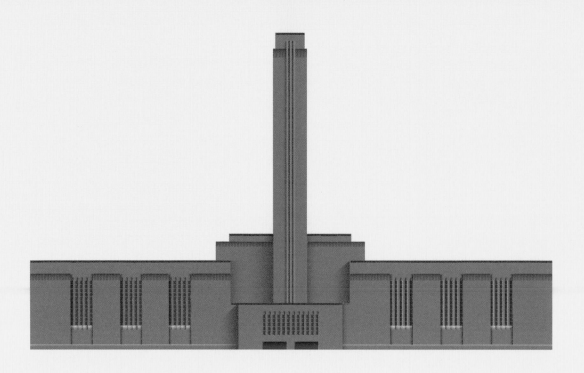

Bankside Power Station
Giles Gilbert Scott

🕐 1963   ◊ SE1 9TG   ↕ 99M

BUS LANE

Bus Lane

First introduced as an experiment on Vauxhall Bridge in 1968, the designated bus lane was an attempt to free London buses from congestion. Today, bus lanes cover much of central London and are shared with taxis and cyclists.

Very few industrial buildings are lucky enough to be preserved, let alone celebrated. **Bankside Power Station (053)**, now home to Tate Modern (103), is a rare exception. But the building wasn't always liked – quite the opposite. It caused controversy from the first proposal. Planned on the South Bank in 1944, its development was in conflict with the desired restructuring of the area for offices, educational and cultural institutions. But the extremely cold winter of 1947, which saw London grind to a standstill amid sweeping power cuts, revealed a growing demand for electricity. The government approved the building against significant opposition from the borough council and local residents.

Architect Giles Gilbert Scott was brought onto the project to address reasonable concerns about the dwarfing of St Paul's Cathedral. He adapted the original plan so in place of two tall chimneys stood one central chimney, which was lowered so as not to exceed the height of St Paul's. This assisted visually, but the relatively short chimney caused pollution problems. In addition, due to temporary shortages of coal (the mining industry was still recovering from the Second World War), the station was redesigned to burn oil instead of coal, which would prove a terrible mistake in the oil crisis of 1973. The station was completed in two stages – the first half opening in 1952 and the second in 1963. It closed only twenty years later.

More exciting additions to the skyline were rising towards the clouds. In quiet Fitzrovia, a technological revolution was under way. The latest exciting addition was the **Post Office Tower (054)** (now the BT Tower). It was built high enough to get a direct line of communication over the Chiltern Hills and up to the next tower in Birmingham. As an important element in the UK's new microwave telecommunications network, built at the height of the Cold War, it was also designed to withstand a nuclear explosion from only a mile away. The cylindrical design was chosen as the most suitable to sustain an atomic blast, as well as strong winds. After construction began, the decision was made to add a viewing platform and rotating restaurant (inspired by a trend from North America and Central Europe). When completed, it became the tallest building in London, beating Battersea Power Station, which at that point was still under construction.

The tower, designated as an official secret due to its strategic importance, could not appear on maps for a long time. This was bizarre, not only because everyone could see the tower from almost everywhere in London, but also because hundreds of thousands of people visited the top. In 1971, a suspected IRA bomb was planted, blasting a large hole in the tower. The viewing platform has been closed ever since, and the restaurant followed suit in 1980. Today, the viewing galleries and former revolving restaurant are still, surprisingly, intact – and are sometimes used for special events and launches.

Hawker Siddeley Harrier

In 1969, the Transatlantic Air Race – between the top of the Post Office Tower in London and the Empire State Building in New York City – was staged. A pilot was hurried on a motorcycle from the tower to St Pancras Station, where a Harrier jump jet was already waiting. After a vertical take-off, he flew across the pond (with some mid-air refuelling). Some six hours later, the airplane landed in Manhattan. The air race was won by the other pilot (in a supersonic Phantom), but it was still a great PR stunt for the new jet.

Austin Mini

These micro-sized cars squeezed into London's traffic jams and became one of the symbols of swinging sixties Britain. Every member of The Beatles had one, as well as 5.4 million other people around the world.

 Post Office Tower
Eric Bedford and G. R. Yeats

🕐 1965 📍 W1T 4JZ ↕ 190M

Centre Point
R. Seifert and Partners

🕐 1966 📍 WC1A 1DD ↕ 117M

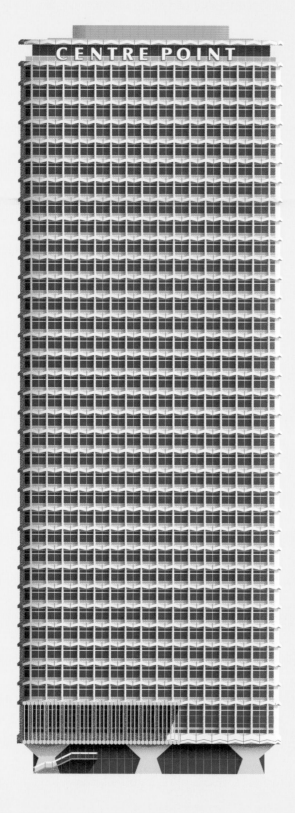

It was not only the government sector, but also the private sector that had pound signs in its eyes during this period. The government relaxed planning laws in a bid to stimulate economic growth and replace jobs in manufacturing. This caused a steep rise of speculative office development in London, on a scale never seen before. Swiss-born Richard Seifert became one of the most economically successful British architects of the century, thanks to his detailed knowledge of planning law and ability to exploit its loopholes and maximise the profits of his clients. His practice R. Seifert and Partners produced designs incredibly fast and completed some 600 buildings around London during his lifetime. The most (in)famous and controversial of Seifert's buildings is **Centre Point (055)**.

The project began when London County Council attempted to buy the land surrounding one of the busiest junctions in central London, where they hoped to build a gyratory system. The landowners were dissatisfied with the money the council was offering and the whole deal stalled. However, the wily property tycoon Harry Hyams took advantage of the delay and bought out all the land right under the council's nose. He then offered the council the space needed for the gyratory in exchange for an allowance for extra high development.

Designed by Seifert's partner George Marsh, Centre Point was constructed between 1963 and 1966. The slender tower has a façade of precast panels, which were hung from the frame without the use of scaffolding – it was the first tall building in London to be constructed this way. The T-shaped panels create a beautiful pop-art pattern, reminiscent of honeycomb. But the street level, typically for Seifert's studio designs, is badly planned and unfriendly to pedestrians.

When the building was finished, the office property market was already saturated. The developer decided to wait for prices to rise and left it empty, including all the flats, for thirteen years during a housing crisis. Its prime location and scale made it the perfect symbol of a property developer's greed. The building was invaded by protestors and squatters a number of times. True to form, it has now been redeveloped into luxury apartments.

Space House (056) was built just a couple of streets away from Centre Point in Holborn. It shares not only the same architect and developer, but also a similar building system. A visually striking and confident façade comprises Y-shaped precast panels, assembled in a circular plan sixteen storeys high. As with other buildings of the practice, the ground level is underwhelming.

But pedestrians were not at the top of the priority list. Car ownership rose dramatically in the 1960s. London's streets were already full of buses, cabs and vans; increasingly affordable cars flooded them. Optimistic town planners, taking cues from Colin Buchanan's influential book *Traffic in Towns*, believed that allocating more space for the traffic would solve congestion, while pedestrians would be safely separated by a system of elevated walkways.

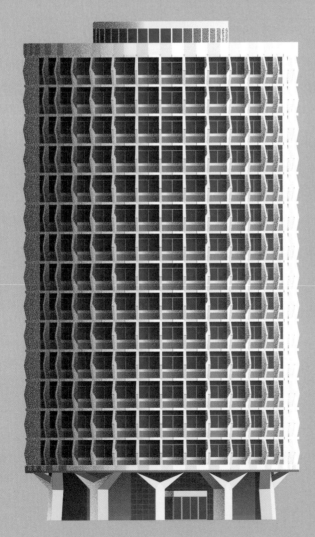

AEC RML Country Bus

The successful Routemaster bus was extended by a row of extra seats, hence the square window in the middle. It is seen here in the green livery of the London Country buses that served the suburbs.

 Space House
R. Seifert and Partners

🕐 1968   ♀ WC2B 4AN

In the 1960s London Bridge was deemed too narrow and it was sold to an American oil tycoon, who rebuilt it in the Arizona desert. Big chunks of the city were demolished to make way for wider roads and roundabouts. Only a lack of money and rising opposition prevented the altogether insane plans from fully materialising. People discovered that wider roads only invited more traffic. Traffic casualties hit an all-time high, and it didn't take long for average speeds to get back to the era of the horse and cart.

The rebuilding of Elephant & Castle was the embodiment of this optimistic traffic planning. Envisaged as the 'Piccadilly Circus of the South', it received a radical makeover. Old streets and buildings were erased. The new **Elephant & Castle Odeon (057)** replaced the 1930s Trocadero 3,000-seat cinema.

It was designed by Ernő Goldfinger, who was responsible for the new office buildings around it, too. It was the only brutalist cinema in London. The cinema had just a third of the seats of the Trocadero cinema it replaced, but this was more than enough in the 1960s, when televisions had invaded the living rooms of most Londoners. The cinema was demolished only twenty-two years later.

Goldfinger was now in demand, after decades of little or no work. However, his name had already become famous, albeit for reasons other than his work. Known for his bad temper, he didn't sit well with his Hampstead neighbour, the writer Ian Fleming, who also disliked Goldfinger's new, modern house. The villain in Fleming's James Bond novel of 1959 was clearly inspired by the architect – not only sharing his name, but also his Eastern European background and Marxist beliefs.

The architect was enraged, but busy with new commissions. Work on new housing in east London finally gave him the chance to put his housing theories in practice. **Balfron Tower (058)** in Poplar is a massive, twenty-six-storey concrete block. The floors are accessible through a separate lift tower, connected by bridges on every third level. Goldfinger had control of both the design and the residency allocation – he had records of all residents, listing their 'suitability' to live in the high-rise building.

Rehousing them by the streets they originally lived in, he tried to keep communities together. On completion of the block, he moved with his wife into a top floor flat for two months. The Goldfingers organised cocktail parties for the tenants as a means of collecting their comments and suggestions. He used this knowledge to design the famous Trellick Tower.

Elephant & Castle Statue

The area takes its name from the sign of a local pub. A statue from the demolished pub was preserved and moved into a new shopping mall in 1965.

Elephant & Castle Odeon
Ernő Goldfinger

🕐 1988   🏛 1957   📍 SE1 6TE

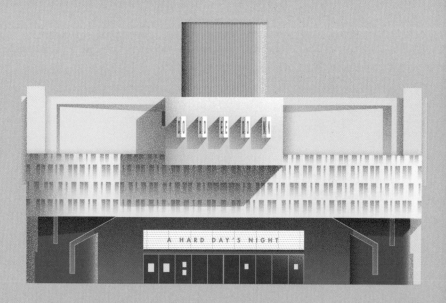

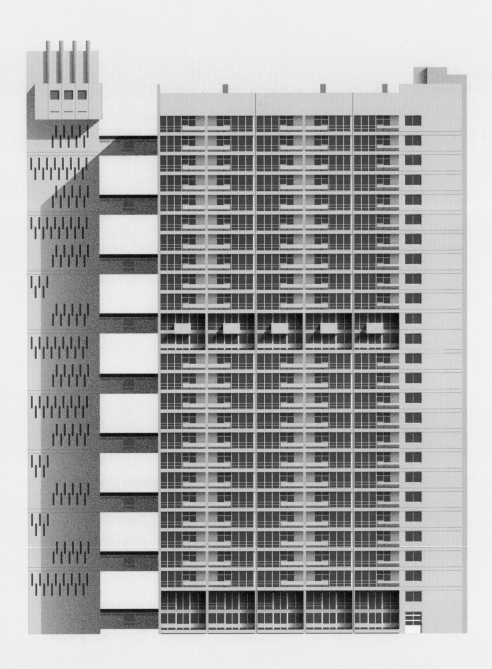

 Balfron Tower
Ernő Goldfinger

🕐 1967 📍 E14 0QR ↕ 84M

US Embassy
Eero Saarinen

🕐 1960   📍 W1A 2LQ

Jaguar 340 3.8

The Metropolitan Police
Service operated a fleet of
Coventry-built Jaguars. Most
of the police cars at the time
were unmarked and only
recognisable by the blue beacon
on the roof. The high-visibility
paint schemes came later.

This was a revolution in terms
of access to housing for the
masses – and elsewhere too
new doctrines were forming and
established orders were being
challenged. World politics was
heating up and protests against
the bloody Vietnam War spread
across the world. The new
US Embassy (059) in Grosvenor
Square, Mayfair, opened just
in time to receive its fair share
of demonstrations. It became
London's first purpose-built
embassy (until then the habit was
to repurpose existing buildings) and
was designed by Finnish-American
architect and designer Eero
Saarinen. The powerful modern
building was inspired by Greek
temples and is strictly symmetrical,
proudly sitting on a podium.

The embassy's scale and modernity,
unseen in Mayfair, proved to be
controversial. It has only six storeys
(plus three underground), but the
width takes over a whole block.
The central entrance is accented
by a bronze eagle with a ten-metre
wing span, balancing on a roof
edge above. The embassy attracted
several mass demonstrations
against the Vietnam War and US
foreign politics and had to be
protected from the crowds by
police cordons. The embassy is
now at the end of its life, as the
US has moved its mission to a
new fortress-like building near the
revived Battersea Power Station
complex. The old Mayfair embassy
is slated to become a luxury hotel.

Kiosk No 8

The new telephone box was introduced in 1968. Architect Bruce Martin simplified the classic No 6 to the bone, so that it was easier to maintain and harder to vandalise.

Hawker Hunter

Pilot Alan Pollock decided to celebrate the fiftieth anniversary of the founding of the RAF in his own way. Angry that the government didn't want to celebrate, he flew his jet around the Houses of Parliament at low level and then, in an incredible stunt, flew through the middle of Tower Bridge.

Victoria Line

The first stage of the new line opened in 1968. It was full of new cutting-edge technology, including automated trains and ticket gates. It was also the first new central Underground line to be built in over sixty years.

Not far from Grosvenor Square is St James Street. **The Economist Buildings (060)** there were designed by husband and wife team Alison and Peter Smithson. An eccentric couple, they dressed in quirky clothes and drove around in an old army Jeep. The Smithsons built relatively few, but important, buildings, which gained them international fame and an almost cult following in Britain. The development for *The Economist* magazine is arguably their best work.

Because the size of the original plot was quite small, the client bought out its neighbours or promised them space in the new development. Instead of replacing the bundle of old buildings with one large tower, the architects designed three smaller blocks that sit around a modest plaza. All this stands on a podium that conceals a car park.

The tallest tower was reserved for the magazine, with the top floor forming a penthouse for the chairperson. The other two towers were reserved for the original occupants of the site – a gentleman's club and a bank. The architecture is unimposing and has aged better than most of its contemporaries. In 1988, it became the first 1960s building in Britain to be listed.

 The Economist Buildings
Alison and Peter Smithson
🕐 1964 📍 SW1A 1HG

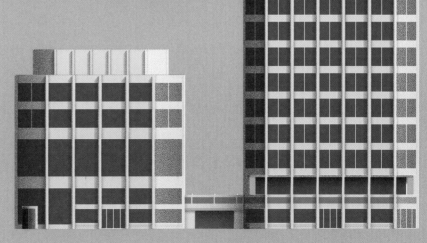

During the 1960s, housing remained a priority. Handsome **Sivill House (061)** in Shoreditch was designed by Berthold Lubetkin and his former colleagues from Tecton. Similar to their previous Spa Green Estate (035) and Hallfield Estate (041), the façade resembles a piece of abstract art and is supposedly inspired by a Caucasian carpet. C-shaped concrete panels decorate the front in a changing rhythm. Although this didn't impress the younger generation of architects, who had already grown weary of the architect's obsession with patterns, believing them a thing of the past. Inside is an extravagant curved central staircase, which one would more readily expect in an upscale mansion than in a council housing project. However, Lubetkin, a life-long communist, believed 'nothing is too good for ordinary people'.

In contrast, many councils built their housing from prefabricated systems with little adaptability. This helped to reduce time on a construction site, since most of the work was undertaken in a factory. The government pushed for the replacement of old housing with new estates, rather than the refurbishment of existing structures.

 Sivill House
Berthold Lubetkin,
Douglas Bailey,
Francis Skinner

🕐 1962   📍 E2 7PH   ↕ 59M

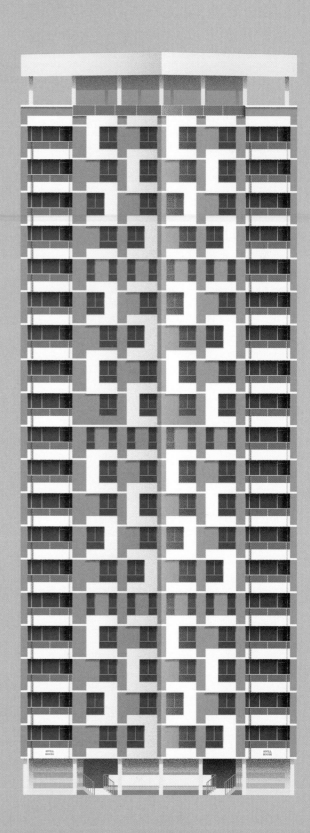

Councils were given subsidies when building high – but there was a problem on the horizon. A gas explosion in a kitchen of a flat in Newham caused the complete collapse of a whole corner of **Ronan Point (062)** tower, which killed four tenants and injured seventeen. Following an investigation, it was revealed that the explosion was relatively minor (the lady preparing her tea survived) and the building was supposed to withstand it. But closer inspection revealed shockingly low standards of construction.

Due to a nationwide shortage of builders, the estates were constructed by an army of mostly unskilled 'assemblers'. In Ronan Point, shoddy work led to defects that left gaps between construction panels — these were then simply covered up by floor boards and wallpaper. The unsound building was, in a bizarre sequence of events, strengthened after the explosion, and the tenants moved back in. But the press latched on to the tragedy and high buildings lost most of their remaining appeal. System building techniques were also revealed to be a big problem, with poor workmanship proving the ultimate source of the tragedy.

 Ronan Point
Newham Council
Architects' Department

1968   E16 3EQ

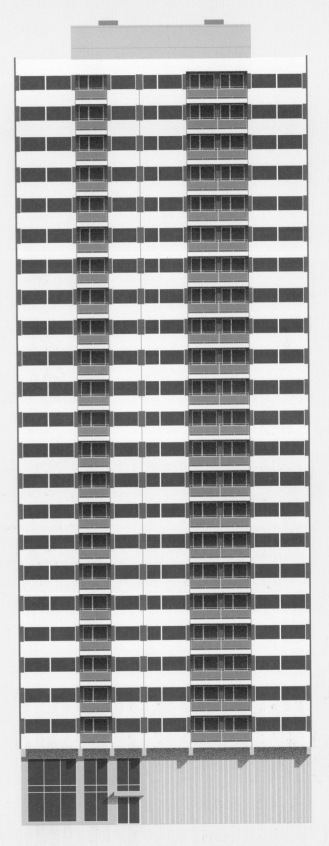

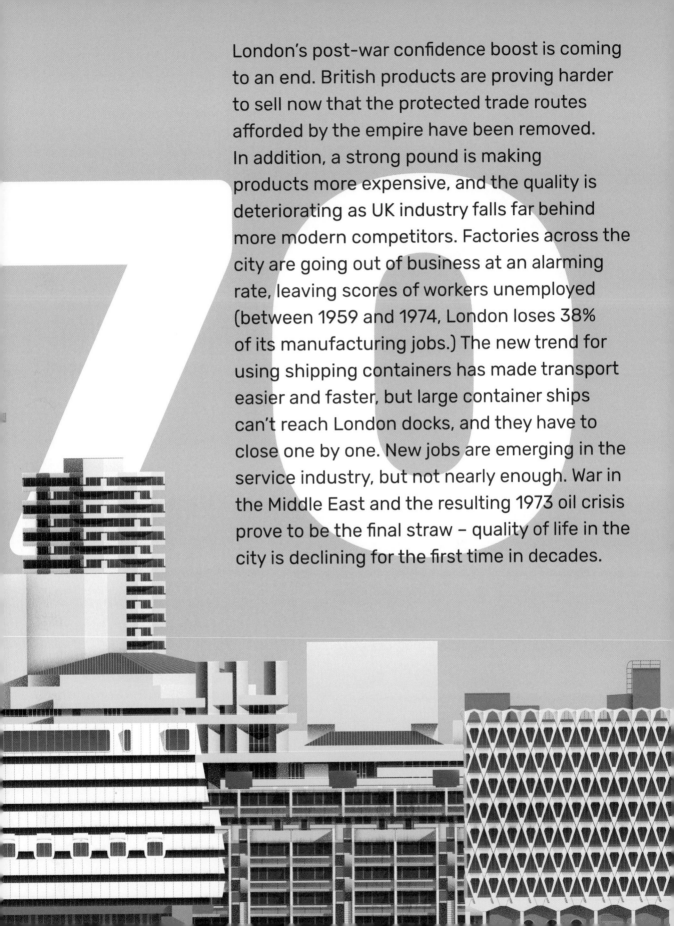

London's post-war confidence boost is coming to an end. British products are proving harder to sell now that the protected trade routes afforded by the empire have been removed. In addition, a strong pound is making products more expensive, and the quality is deteriorating as UK industry falls far behind more modern competitors. Factories across the city are going out of business at an alarming rate, leaving scores of workers unemployed (between 1959 and 1974, London loses 38% of its manufacturing jobs.) The new trend for using shipping containers has made transport easier and faster, but large container ships can't reach London docks, and they have to close one by one. New jobs are emerging in the service industry, but not nearly enough. War in the Middle East and the resulting 1973 oil crisis prove to be the final straw – quality of life in the city is declining for the first time in decades.

063 NLA Tower
R. Seifert and Partners

🕐 1970   📍 CR0 0XT   ↕ 82M

Croydon was an area that saw significant post-war development, earning it the (slightly sarcastic) nickname of 'mini Manhattan'; its high-rise towers and car-friendly streets were the work of James Marshall, the authoritarian leader of Croydon Council who hoped to capitalise on the building boom. Many corporations took advantage of the cheap land and limited planning restrictions, relocating there from central London.

Richard Seifert's practice added the **NLA Tower (063)** (now No 1 Croydon) to the skyline. It became known locally as 'the wedding cake' or '50p building', in response to its layered storeys and trimmed edges. The tower was originally planned as part of a larger development, but a single homeowner refused to sell her house. As a result, the building had to squeeze onto the middle of a roundabout. The resulting geometric beauty is arguably one of R. Seifert and Partners' best works.

Jubilee Line

In 1977, Britain celebrated Queen Elizabeth II's Silver Jubilee, marking twenty-five years on the throne. Subsequently, the name of a new Underground line was changed from the Fleet Line (after the River Fleet) to Jubilee. It officially opened in 1979.

Guy's Tower
W. H. Watkins, Gray and Partners
🕐 1974   📍 SE1 9RT   ↕ 142M

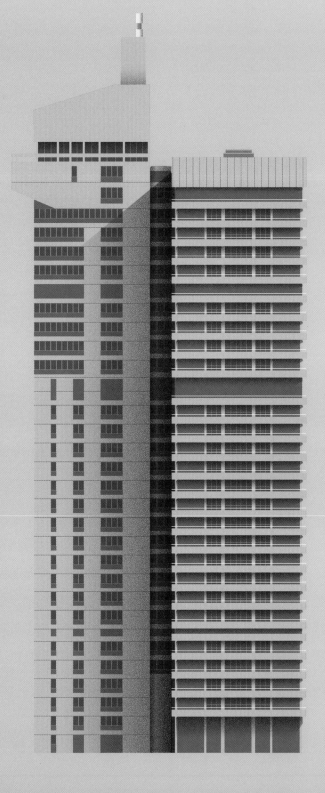

Back in the City, the new
Guy's Tower (064) rose to an
incredible 142 metres. The tower
opened in 1974 and became the
tallest hospital in the world.
It kept the title until 1990, probably
because it's not exactly the most
practical layout for a hospital.
The building is actually made
of two parts. A plain block with
strip windows is connected to
the service tower, which has
a strange bulge of a lecture
theatre on the top floor. In 2014,
it was badly weathered and the
concrete façade was reclad with
'fancy' aluminium panels, which
incidentally make it look worse.

Amid a declining quality of
life, dismay in London grew.
Unemployment rose dramatically,
as did prices – in 1975, inflation
reached 25%. The economy was
crippled by massive strikes by
powerful trade unions, and the
government had to introduce
a three-day week in order to
save energy. Streets and parks
were flooded with rubbish, as
waste collectors went on strike.
Meanwhile, the conflict in Northern
Ireland grew bloodier. The violence
had begun in the 1960s, but at this
point was barely making headlines
in the UK. Irish Republicans
decided to change all that and
began a bombing campaign
on London, in the belief that
spreading fear and terror would
force the government to retreat
its advances on Northern Ireland.

But while the language of the gun was how some did business, old-fashioned diplomacy was also still a powerful force, and other countries wanted a new embassy just like the US (see 059). The **Czechoslovak Embassy (065)** in Kensington offered the central European country the opportunity to present itself and its rich architectural history (of which it was particularly proud) to an international audience. The project started in 1965 and remained on track for completion even after the country was invaded by Soviet forces three years later.

A team of progressive architects was led by Jan Šrámek – they went on to design a number of embassies around the globe. In London, they joined forces with Robert Matthew, one of the architects of the Royal Festival Hall (036). Critics admired the quality of the work and technical detail, and in 1971 the building was unanimously voted by RIBA as the best work by a foreign architect in the UK. Back in Czechoslovakia, people linked the new brutalist buildings with the growingly oppressive communist regime and were (and still are) far from appreciative of them.

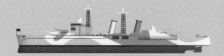

HMS Belfast

The almost 200-metre-long cruiser served with the Royal Navy in the Second World War and the Korean War. After it was decommissioned, it was moored between Tower and London Bridge and became a museum ship in 1971.

Hughes 300

The nimble American helicopter was operated by the first British female commercial helicopter pilot, Gay Absalom Barrett. She flew missions for the Metropolitan Police in the early 1970s.

(065) **Czechoslovak Embassy**
Jan Bočan,
Jan Šrámek,
Robert Matthew

🕐 1970   📍 W8 4QY

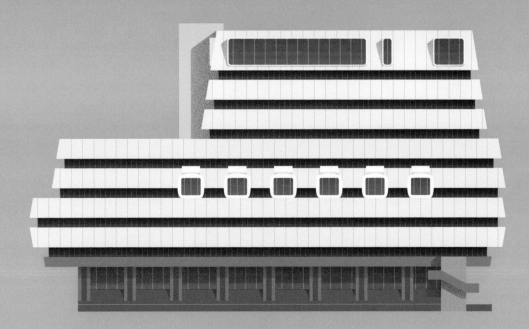

Prince Charles had a similar opinion on almost any new building, and rallying against modern architecture became one of his pastimes when off royal duty. He used his connections and influence to sabotage a number of modern developments, most notably the extension of the National Gallery. The Darth Vader of modern architecture branded **Mondial House (066)** 'a word processor' (early computer), which was a surprisingly close call – it being the main telecommunications hub in the country.

The futuristic concrete structure was clad in pristine glass-reinforced polystyrene panels, which stayed bright even after thirty years. Built in the middle of the Cold War, the bomb-proof building was specifically designed with protection in mind (it being strategically very important) – it had backup generators, hence the six cooling cubes on the roof. Sitting on the banks of the River Thames, its floors sloped down towards the riverbank, so as not to obstruct the view of St Paul's Cathedral (like its predecessor the Faraday Building (026) had done forty years earlier). Technology developed with incredible speed, and the equipment inside soon became obsolete. In 2005, to Prince Charles' relief, the building was demolished.

MONDIAL HOUSE

**Contemporary lettering
cast in concrete**

Only a few architects managed to be both admired and loathed during their lifetime. Basil Spence was one of them. The Scottish architect became known after winning a major competition for the new Coventry Cathedral, the original having been destroyed in the Blitz. While busy working on a pavilion for the Festival of Britain, he designed the cathedral as an evening project. His unconventional design was disliked by the public, the press and even Coventry Council itself. Nevertheless, the cathedral was constructed, and most people grew to like it after a couple of decades.

Spence's **Hyde Park Barracks (067)** proved to be controversial as well. The home of the Household Cavalry, the barracks are just a short horse ride away from Buckingham Palace, where the cavalry conducts ceremonial duties. The long, narrow site on which Spence's building now stands had been occupied by the cavalry since 1795, and by this point they were fast outgrowing it. Spence was asked to squeeze in new quarters and a mess hall to accommodate 500 soldiers, along with stables for 273 horses – all while leaving enough space for parade grounds where the soldiers and horses could train.

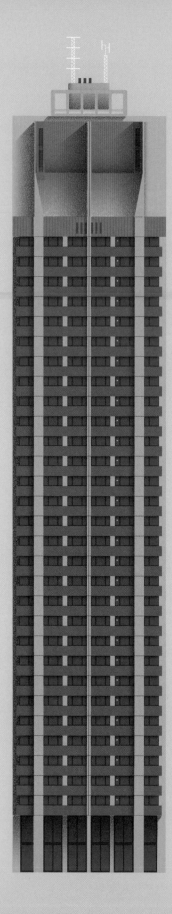

The architect's solution was to build a thirty-three-storey tower and couple it with additional lower blocks. He reasoned that the tall and slender tower wouldn't block views of the park or cast a large shadow, which a lower and wider building slab would. The downside, of course, is that it is much more visible from the park.

Not far away is another Spence work – **50 Queen Anne's Gate (068)** was built on the site of Queen Anne's Mansions, dating from 1877. The original building was extremely tall for its time and blocked views of the Houses of Parliament from Buckingham Palace. As a result, legislation limiting building height was introduced. There wasn't much opposition when the unloved building was demolished in the early 1970s. But its replacement garnered outrage again, which uncommonly united the public and the political establishment. Spence, who was the design consultant on the project, was even accused by MPs of providing deceptive drawings.

(067) **Hyde Park Barracks**
Basil Spence

🕐 1970   📍 SW7 1SE   ↕ 94M

The massive, top-heavy concrete building is reminiscent of a fortress, rather than offices. Perhaps suitably, it was a base for the Home Office, which was responsible for everything from security to immigration. Its workers nicknamed the building 'the Lubyanka', after the headquarters of the KGB in Moscow. Unfortunately, Spence – no doubt hurt by the mounting rude remarks – died just as the construction was coming to an end.

The Home Office moved in 2005, relocating to new, purpose-built headquarters designed by Terry Farrell. The empty building was refurbished and renamed 102 Petty France. It is now home to the Ministry of Justice.

AEC Routemaster

In 1977, London was captivated by the massive celebrations surrounding Queen Elizabeth II's Silver Jubilee. A batch of Routemaster buses were painted silver for the occasion.

 (068) **50 Queen Anne's Gate**
Basil Spence

🕐 1976   📍 SW1H 9AJ

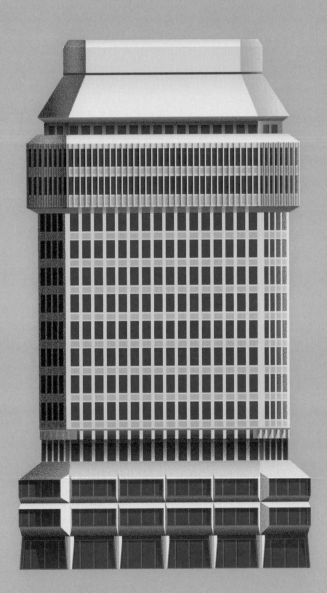

 (069) **Welbeck Street Car Park**
Michael Blampied and Partners
🕐 1971   📍 W1G 0BB

Oxford Austin 1300

Most of the Metropolitan Police Service's cars up until this point had been painted black, without any markings. When the new colour scheme was introduced, people nicknamed them 'panda cars'.

More controversial concrete appeared near Oxford Street, London's main shopping street. The new Debenhams department store had to build its own parking facilities, as was requested by car-friendly planners of the time. **Welbeck Street Car Park (069)**, with a 400-vehicle capacity, was built just across the road. When finished, the car park attracted more coverage in the architecture press than the actual store.

Its impressive façade is made from interlocked V-shaped concrete units that are also load-bearing, thus removing the need for internal columns – very useful in a car park. Nevertheless, the space was very rarely used – people preferred on-street parking and the area had good public transport links. The building is currently awaiting demolition, despite a lot of support from modernist advocates, as the ground has become increasingly valuable. It is to be replaced by a hotel.

Extension of the Underground to Heathrow

London's largest airport was finally connected with the London Underground network in 1977 when Queen Elizabeth II opened the new Piccadilly Line extension.

Over in the City, more buildings kept rising. The triangle site of **30 Cannon Street (070)** was one of the last Second World War bomb sites to be redeveloped, not least because of its challenging proportions. The building's distinctive façade is made from ultra-modern panels (a mix of fibreglass and cement), which hide a clever drainage system that keeps the surface clean. The lightness of these panels allowed the architects to design external walls sloping outwards in five-degree angles, making every floor larger than the one below.

Revolutionary at the time (and built for a French bank), it is now fairly common to add extra floor space like this — although with less elegance (see the Walkie Talkie (116)). The glazing itself was tinted bronze, which went some way to shading the interiors. Tinted glass was quite popular during the 1970s, but practically disappeared with the improvement of air conditioning systems and a growing desire for uninterrupted views. Forty years on, the building still looks remarkably modern, unlike the majority of the commercial buildings of this era, which were largely demolished and replaced. It has also been recently refurbished – the dated window glazing now replaced with clear glass.

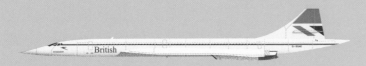

Concorde

The supersonic airliner was a British-French design that operated from Heathrow from 1976 to 2003. It immediately became an icon and its silhouette even decorates the Heathrow Terminals 1, 2 and 3 Underground station.

(070) **30 Cannon Street**
Whinney, Son and Austen Hall

🕐 1977 📍 EC4M 6YQ

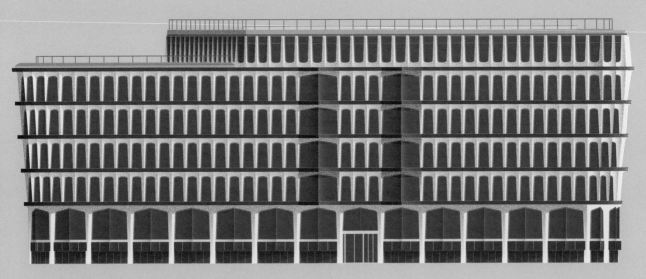

Elevated housing was still being built in the 1970s, even after its heyday had waned. **Grenfell Tower (071)** in North Kensington was built as a part of the Lancaster West Estate. There was already strong opposition to building new housing in the form of tower blocks, but the need to squeeze as many flats onto a site as possible demanded it. The chief architect of the estate, Clifford Wearden, disliked Grenfell Tower, but nonetheless viewed it as a necessary evil.

In the wake of the Ronan Point tragedy (062), the structure was designed with extra strength in mind. It even featured external concrete columns, something unseen on similar buildings. The ground floor was used as a car park, and the first three floors were designed as commercial units in a bid to encourage local business and to replicate the settings of more organic residential communities.

One summer night in 2017, a fire broke out in a tenant's kitchen. The residents were instructed to remain in their flats and wait for rescue. This is standard practice in concrete tower blocks, which are specifically designed to contain fires in the affected unit. Unfortunately, the fire breached the confines of the flat and soon spread, engulfing the entire façade. An estimated seventy-one people perished that night.

A preliminary investigation brought some shocking facts to light: Kensington and Chelsea Council had ignored repeated warnings from residents calling for a review of fire safety. During the refurbishment, the council, despite being one of the richest boroughs in the country, had pushed for the cheapest suppliers and materials possible. As a result, the building was clad in a combustible material, which was only slightly cheaper than the alternative fireproof option.

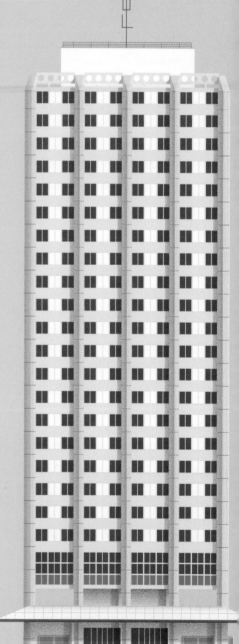

Beagle Pup

In 1973 a City worker accused of fraud was released on bail. He rented this airplane and flew it between the City towers and even through London Bridge. He continued up north, before eventually crashing into a forest.

 (071) **Grenfell Tower**
Clifford Wearden
and Associates

🕐 1974   📍 W11 1TQ   ↕ 67M

Located in the same borough and designed around the same time as Grenfell Tower, the **World's End Estate (072)** is surprisingly different. The architects, Eric Lyons (famous for his modernist Span estates) and Jim Cadbury-Brown, did their best to avoid the mistakes made on high-rise estates of the previous decade. Named after a local pub, the estate was designed for an extremely high population density, almost twice the maximum permitted by London County Council. Plans had initially been rejected and were only passed after a public inquiry, which appreciated the quality of the proposal.

Around half of the dwellings are organised into seven high-rise towers of varying heights. The rest of the tenants are spread across low-rise blocks that connect each of the towers, effectively creating one large building. The warm-brick façade stands in contrast to the concrete monoliths of the era, and the polygonal structure helps break down the scale and resulting monotony – two aspects particularly disliked by residents of other estates. It is now a desired place to live and, incredibly, most of the 750 flats are still rented from the council.

World's End Estate
Jim Cadbury-Brown
& Eric Lyons

🕐 1977 📍 SW10 0EH

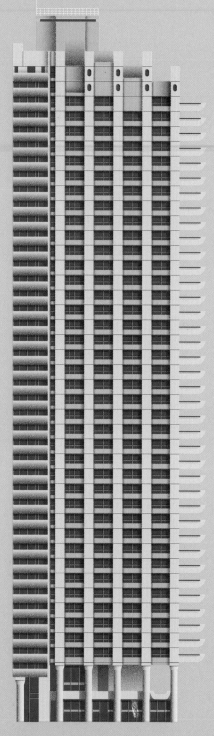

The Barbican is one of the most impressive and successful post-war developments in the world. The competition for its design was won by Chamberlin, Powell and Bon who had just finished Golden Lane Estate (043) on the neighbouring site. It was clear from the very start that this was not social housing, but a place for the middle and higher classes – reflected in its construction budget and resulting rents.

The City was practically empty after the war and the estate was intent on luring people back. Architects designed a vast, car-free complex dominated by three high-rises, including **Shakespeare Tower (073)**. The trio became the tallest residential buildings in Europe. The massive scale of the Barbican complex, alongside numerous builders' strikes and design tweaks, meant that construction took decades. Barbican Centre (080), one of the last parts to be completed, opened in 1982.

But the wait was worth it – it remains one of the most staggering feats of residential design in the world. A rare example of a working 'city within a city', the estate is such that residents theoretically never have to leave. Restaurants, shops, parks, an arts centre, a library and even schools form part of the complex.

The original plan saw the Barbican's walkways connected with a larger system of elevated walkways proposed by the City, named the 'Pedway' system. These walkways were intended to stretch right across the City (to the extent that all new buildings had to incorporate street access to the first floor, the NatWest Tower (077) included). Budget cuts – and common sense – meant that the plans were never fully realised.

Daimler Fleetline

London Transport was short of funds and introduced buses operated only by a driver, to save on the salaries of bus conductors. But the buses weren't reliable and their maintenance proved expensive. After a few years, they disappeared from London's streets.

(073) **Shakespeare Tower**
Chamberlin, Powell and Bon
🕐 1973   📍 EC2Y 8DD

The less glamorous council housing at **Robin Hood Gardens (074)** in Poplar was the product of theoretical work from Alison and Peter Smithson, architects of the outstanding Economist Buildings (060). They developed the design around the concept of 'streets in the sky', which had been tried a few times before (with varied success) by other contemporary architects. Wide open walkways provided access to the flats and were supposed to imitate the social life of the actual streets they replaced. But unlike real streets, they weren't overlooked by residents (the flats backed onto them) and were mostly empty – purely because tenants were spread on different floors and population density was quite low.

The unsupervised space was ideal for vandals and burglars, while the council seriously neglected maintenance and left the buildings to slowly fall apart. Residents' complaints were twenty times higher than at other Greater London Council estates. The estate was also hemmed in by a busy dual carriageway on three sides. The architects designed a number of clever solutions to limit the noise, including concrete vertical ribs that stopped the sound from travelling over the façade. Another solution was to hide the estate behind a high concrete wall, although this unfortunately isolated the complex.

But by and large the flats would have been envied by most; innovative layouts were generously sized and full of sun. Unfortunately, the rise of nearby Canary Wharf and other commercial pressures accelerated the estate's demise. Plans were approved to replace the original 252 flats with over 1,500 new homes. Just as the demolition started in late 2017, the Victoria and Albert Museum salvaged a whole three-storey section of the building with the intention to display it.

Commer FC Van

Vans in this dazzling livery were zooming through the streets every day delivering the *London Evening Standard*, the city's biggest newspaper.

 Robin Hood Gardens
Alison and Peter Smithson

🕐 1972   📍 E14 0HG

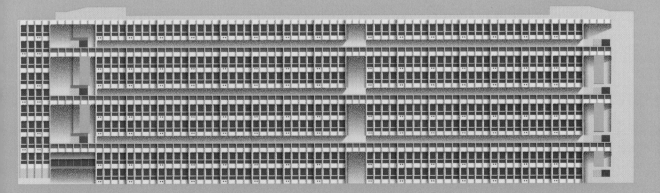

Further north, Camden Council was very progressive, its architecture department led by Sydney Cook. Cook believed in an alternative to high-rise towers and headhunted the best architects with a similar ethos. Neave Brown – born in New York and who sadly passed away at the start of 2018 – became perhaps the most well-known of them all. Brown believed he could achieve the housing density of high-rise towers, while keeping the street fabric and building low-rise. **Alexandra Road Estate (075)** is one of the most ambitious housing projects of its time. The concrete megastructure, stretching 300 metres along the railway line, has stepped terraces, forming a ziggurat-type structure.

This permits every flat direct access to the 'street', which cuts across the complex and is overlooked by residents' windows. As a result, the estate had the lowest level of vandalism in the entire borough. Unfortunately, unforeseen issues with the foundations and extraordinarily high inflation rates in the 1970s tripled the costs. A public inquiry into the project revealed that Brown was not responsible for the spiralling costs, but his reputation in Britain nevertheless took a major hit. Unable to find work, he turned to projects in the Netherlands. Thankfully, his genius was reappraised, and forty years later he became the first architect in Britain to have all of his buildings listed.

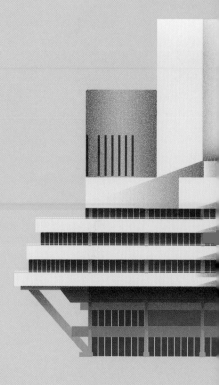

 Alexandra Road Estate
Neave Brown

🕑 1978   ♀ NW8 0SN

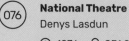 **National Theatre**
Denys Lasdun

🕑 1976   ♀ SE1 9PX

Cultural buildings bloomed in the 1970s, particularly libraries and theatres. Plans for a new National Theatre for London had been in place since the end of the Second World War, and in 1951 a foundation stone was laid on the South Bank. However, problems with funding meant the construction didn't start until 1969. A board of theatre directors, designers and technical experts was set up to select an architectural team. The board met with many different studios, each of whom brought a large team of experts in a bid to prove their worth and experience. Denys Lasdun was the only one to show up alone, and he reportedly confessed to knowing very little about theatre design.

Nevertheless, his vision and notorious persistence in the study of design and function impressed the board enough that he was selected. Lasdun spent more than a decade researching, designing and building the **National Theatre (076)**.

It consists of three separate auditoria, which are loosely based on theatre designs from the greatest periods of drama – namely classical Greek theatres, Tudor inn-yards and more modern theatres of the preceding three centuries. The architect compared the design process to planning a small city, in which a number of elements need to work together.

Some of his solutions were unorthodox though, and had to be amended in subsequent years. The exterior is characterised by vertical stage towers (that hide a rope system for each stage) and a sequence of horizontal terraces. Prince Charles, of course, felt obliged to comment and compared it to a nuclear power station.

It was too modern for some, but for architecture critics it was outdated. In 1976, concrete was already out of fashion and buildings so bold and confident seemed inappropriate in a time of economic uncertainty. But today it is seen by many as a brutalist masterpiece shining with high-quality craftsmanship.

At the start of the 1980s, Margaret Thatcher – the UK's first female prime minister – is in power. The desperate economic situation of the 1970s has encouraged huge reforms (changes that will have an effect on the nation for generations to come). London – particularly the City – is benefitting greatly from these changes, while other parts of the country, such as Wales, are hit hard. State-owned companies are being privatised and once powerful workers' unions systematically dismantled. The deregulation of the financial markets will soon lead to the 'Big Bang', encouraging an influx in foreign investment and a rebooting of the economy. As a result, the cityscape is set to experience a radical transformation.

The new decade opened with the **NatWest Tower (077)** (now Tower 42), the first London skyscraper by international standards. Designed in the late 1960s and constructed through the 1970s, it was already dated when it eventually opened. The planning process was heated, and the planning approval controversial due to the building's extraordinary height. But this was Richard Seifert, who knew all the tricks. The tower was intended to encourage the further building of tall skyscrapers in the capital, but it remained the tallest building in the City for thirty years (until Heron Tower (114) was built).

The tower has a large core, which supports three cantilevered 'leaves', containing the actual office space. This was structurally innovative but also quite wasteful, since the floor area was smaller than for a traditional tower of half the height. The tower's floorplan mimics the bank's logo, although the architect maintained it was a coincidence. The tenant wasn't entirely satisfied with the much delayed new building, as it wasn't large enough to house the whole company. After it was severely damaged in an IRA bombing in 1993, NatWest never returned, instead relocating to the new Broadgate development (p.102).

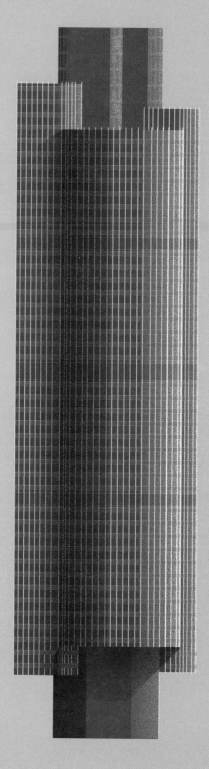

(077) **NatWest Tower**
R. Seifert and Partners
🕐 1980 ◊ EC2N 1HQ ↕ 199M

But the most striking headquarters building of this period was surely that of Lloyd's. **The Lloyd's Building (078)** is one of the most well-known modern London landmarks. Designed by Florence-born Richard Rogers, it shares a philosophy with his previous building – the Centre Georges Pompidou in Paris, which he designed with Italian architect Renzo Piano. The building is unusual in positioning its services, such as lifts, staircases, water pipes and air ducts, on the outside, leaving a free uncluttered internal space. In concept, this was practical for maintenance and upgrade.

In reality, everything is exposed to the elements and gets rusty and dirty, making the impressive building expensive to upkeep. Six towers flank a central rectangular space. The ultra-modern interior features a dining room from 1756, which was transported directly from the old Lloyd's Building piece by piece. The front façade of the earlier building was also preserved and was left free standing on one side (the rest of the building was demolished to make way for the new construction). Open-plan offices share a sixty-metre-high lobby, a source of plentiful natural light. Its unusual design makes the building a regular backdrop in sci-fi films such as *Guardians of the Galaxy* (2014).

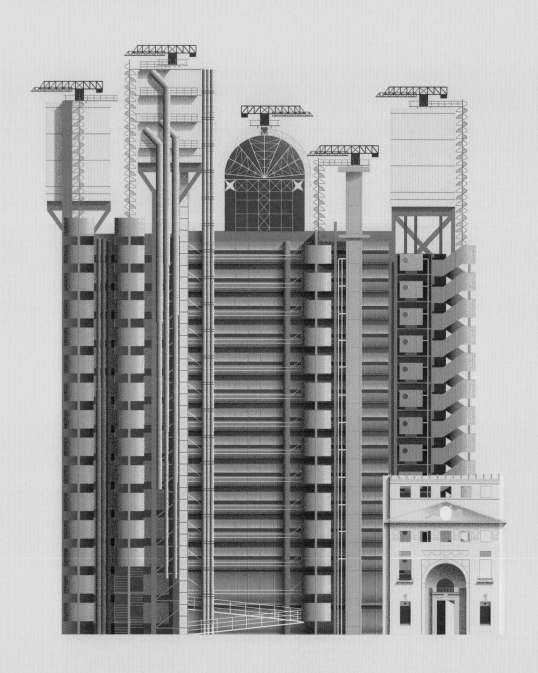

The Lloyd's Building

078 Richard Rogers and Partners

🕐 1986   📍 EC3M 7HA   ↕ 95M

Growing demand for office space led to an 'over spilling' of new developments beyond the City borders. **No 1 London Bridge (079)** stands on the south side of London Bridge, facing the once super-modern Adelaide House (003) across the river. Its flat, glossy surface and stainless steel details make for a somewhat sterile appearance. Surprisingly, the building was constructed from precast panels, delivered from the factory already cladded and with windows fitted, leaving only the assembly once the panels were on site.

To soften the scale of the fairly large building, the bulk is split into three parts of varying height. The tallest, a thirteen-storey tower, is connected with a lower block by a glazed link sloping towards the river. The building's corner touching the bridgehead is cut to offer a view of the City (presumably so the workers inside still feel part of the show).

Rover SD1

Budget controls meant that most Metropolitan Police vehicles were now coated in the cheapest colour – white – and only had a strip of colour. The cars were soon nicknamed the 'jam sandwich'.

 No 1 London Bridge
John S. Bonnington Partnership

🕐 1986   📍 SE1 9BG

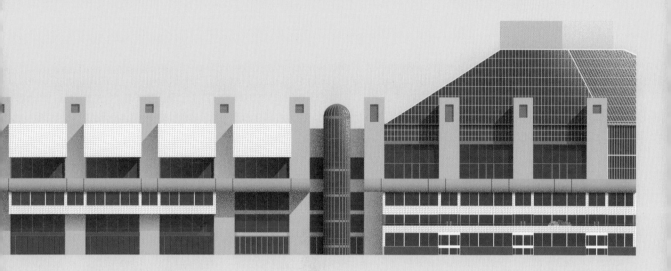

Barbican Centre
Chamberlin, Powell and Bon

🕐 1982 📍 EC2Y 8DS

Kiosk KX100

The state-run department for post and telecommunications was privatised in the 1980s and split into the Post Office and British Telecommunications (BT). Part of the new investment was an updated series of minimalist telephone boxes.

While new office buildings sprung up all around it, the finishing touches were being made to the **Barbican Centre (080)**, ending the thirty-year construction process of the Barbican complex. Most of the residential buildings had been completed in the 1970s (see Shakespeare Tower (073)), but the Centre itself took more than a decade to build. During this time, a number of revisions were made to introduce further cultural functions. Ultimately, these changes made the navigation of the Centre very confusing, especially for new visitors. But once oriented, one notices the amazing level of detail and the quality of the materials used throughout the building.

The two main entertainment venues – the concert hall and the theatre auditorium – are buried underground. As with the National Theatre (076), the stage tower pierces the roof. There, it is surrounded by a glazed structure, which forms a massive tropical conservatory. The Barbican Centre has become a favourite cultural hotspot among Londoners, thanks to its generous mix of gallery spaces, a library, restaurants and bars, all spread across a vast and architecturally impressive site. It has more recently become a centre point in the rediscovery (and renewed admiration) of brutalism by the general public.

During the Thatcher years, construction of council housing was effectively stopped – it was believed that the free market would do the job of providing housing. In addition, the government introduced the 'Right to Buy' scheme, whereby tenants were offered the chance to buy their council-allocated homes at a large discount, while the councils themselves were forbidden from reinvesting in new housing. By the end of the 1970s, more than 40% of Britons lived in council homes, including both low-income and middle-class families. The 1980s marked the beginning of a transformation in the residential make-up of central London. The age of the luxury housing market was dawning.

One of the first instances of upmarket development occurred in the Docklands area – once a source of London's wealth, the Docklands now stood empty. Large storage warehouses in the Bermondsey area were successfully converted into trendy lofts, in response to a new-found love of the river – the once 'biologically dead' and foul-smelling river of previous decades had been brought back to life by London's improved sewage system and the introduction of important environmental legislation in the 1970s.

China Wharf (081) was one of the first of Bermondsey's residential redevelopments. Andrew Wadsworth, a developer in his early twenties, teamed up with Brighton-born architect Piers Gough of CZWG. The new, river-facing building features three very different façades, each designed in reaction to their immediate surroundings. The wall adjoining a neighbouring warehouse is clad in brick, while the courtyard façade is made from concrete flutes that mimic grain silos, prominent features of the dock's past.

Thames Barrier

London is so close to the North Sea that a combination of high tides and increased river flow can easily cause floods. The massive, rotating steel barriers of the Thames Barrier have been protecting the city since 1984.

 China Wharf
CZWG

🕐 1988   📍 SE1 2BQ

(082) **The Circle**
CZWG

🕐 1989   ◇ SE1 2JE

MCW Metrocab

A new taxi model was introduced in 1987. Although it had some success, most of the cabbies decided to stick with their ageing FX4s. There are still some Metrocabs operating in London, although they are quickly becoming a rarity.

In contrast, the riverfront side is bright red and glazed with large curved windows. A central balcony on the lowest floor takes the shape of a blue boat, seemingly floating under the building – typical of postmodern humour. The jokes don't end there either; the building is not named, as one might think, after the oriental connections fostered by the River Thames. It's simply named after the developer's cat.

The Circle (082) is just a couple of streets away; this time more straightforwardly named after the courtyard created at its centre. Built by the same team, it shares both the postmodern wit and boldness of China Wharf. A large complex with more than 300 flats is dominated by four towers adorned in glazed blue tiles. Their shape was reportedly inspired by vases, although most people compare them to owls. Strikingly, the balconies run diagonally over the façade, bizarrely supported by thick wooden logs, although the flats themselves are surprisingly ordinary.

Leyland Titan Docklands Express

The new bus line provided additional links to the previously inaccessible Docklands. Proposals for further extensions to the Jubilee Line were dragging as developers and TfL argued over who should finance them.

 Shadwell Basin Housing
MacCormac, Jamieson, Prichard and Wright

🕐 1988 📍 E1W 3SG

Shadwell Basin Housing (083) in Wapping was built in 1988. Unlike most docks in the area, which had been drained and landfilled, Shadwell Dock was left with water. It became a place for recreational sailing, canoeing and even swimming. Because of this, plans for proposed housing around the basin's edge had to be altered in order not to obstruct the wind required for sailing. The London Docklands Development Corporation (LDDC), responsible for the redevelopment of the area, split larger sites and commissioned different architects to bring variety into the redevelopment.

LDDC specified the use of 'traditional' London stock bricks and slate roofs in all the designs, but Shadwell Basin is traditional only in material. The playful façades, inspired by local warehouse architecture, have portholes, archways and unusual gables split in two: features that do well to integrate the large development into its surroundings. Architects also modelled the houses into rows, attempting to disguise the large development as terrace houses.

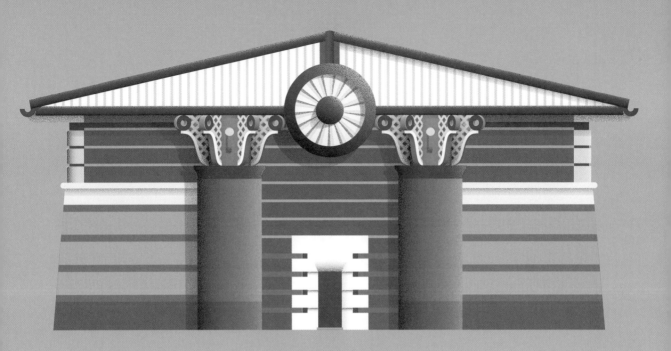

 (084) **Isle of Dogs Pumping Station**
John Outram

🕐 1988   📍 E14 3YH

Docklands Light Railway

The DLR opened in 1987 as a much needed transport link between the City and Canary Wharf. Its capacity was relatively small and had to be extended immediately after opening.

New infrastructure was required to cope with growing development demands in London's Docklands. The **Isle of Dogs Pumping Station (084)** designed by John Outram is one of the most playful buildings of the 1980s. It's one of three pumping stations commissioned from prestigious architects – the other two being Norman Foster and Nicholas Grimshaw.

Outram, well known for ancient references in his work, nicknamed the building a 'Temple of Storms', its function being to pump flood water into the River Thames. The building's colourful decoration is not just for show either, and plays a central role in the building's function. Two huge columns cleverly conceal ventilation ducts, and the central 'eye' forms a fan, essential for preventing a dangerous build-up of methane gas. Even Prince Charles was a fan.

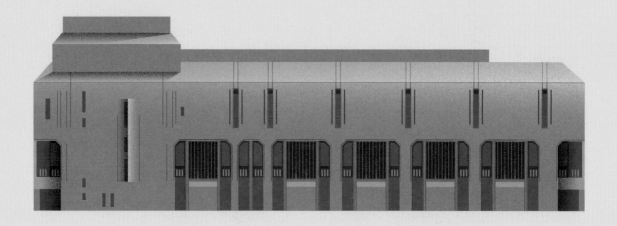

Ismaili Centre
Casson Conder Partnership

🕐 1985   📍 SW7 2SL

Far from London's Docklands, in a much more chi chi neighbourhood, the **Ismaili Centre (085)** was built as a religious and cultural meeting place of the UK Ismaili community. Its prominent site, facing the Victoria and Albert Museum, was originally set aside for a new National Theatre building (076), but it was deemed too small and became a car hire parking lot, before being purchased by the community.

The brief was to design a 'London building' that didn't have to follow traditions of Islamic architecture, but which would retain the feel of it. The architects didn't copy or reference any existing Islamic buildings, and went on to incorporate an eclectic combination of elements from both Islamic and Western architecture. The building has traditional details such as teak-framed bow windows, but is definitively modern overall.

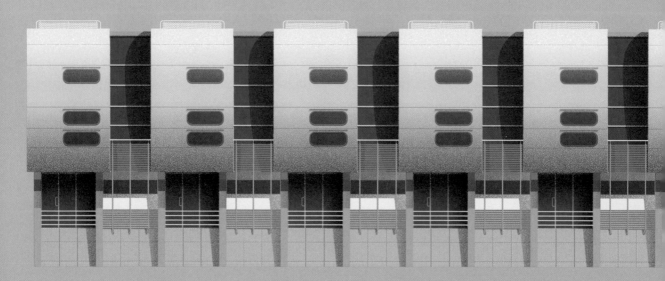

Bell 222

In 1980 the Metropolitan Police finally bought their own helicopters, after decades of renting them from private operators. The helicopter unit was based in Lippitts Hill, Essex, just a short flight from London.

de Havilland Canada Dash 7

To prove that plans for the new City airport were plausible, a test flight of this aircraft took place in 1982. The airplane landed on the site of today's Heron Quays station, much to the surprise to many doubters who couldn't believe 1,000 metres was enough for a landing strip.

That said, it is nothing compared to the 'space architecture' of **Grand Union Canal Housing (086)**, which was built on a narrow strip of land parallel to the Grand Union Canal. Forming part of a major redevelopment in the Camden area, the houses constitute a section of a large complex commissioned by the retail giant Sainsbury's, which also includes a supermarket, school, office space and parking area. The entire development was designed by English architect Nicholas Grimshaw, who was able to negotiate a series of individual houses and maisonettes rather than the go-to 'block' of flats.

Well known for this high-tech architecture style, Grimshaw designed eleven aluminium-clad houses, which are nestled tightly between the supermarket's loading bay and the canal. Since the houses have no south-facing wall, they are top-lit with an angled skylight that distributes light through a two-storey atrium. The ultra-modern aesthetic is completed by electronically operated glazed window walls that open from the living room out onto the terrace.

(086) **Grand Union Canal Housing**
Nicholas Grimshaw

🕐 1988 📍 NW1 9LP

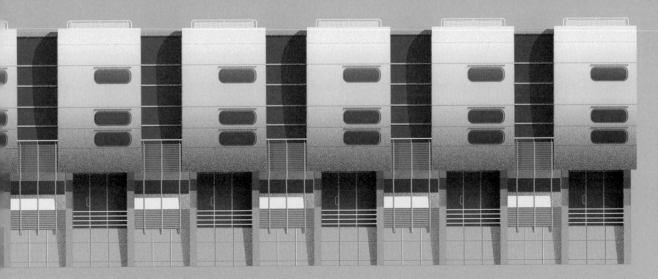

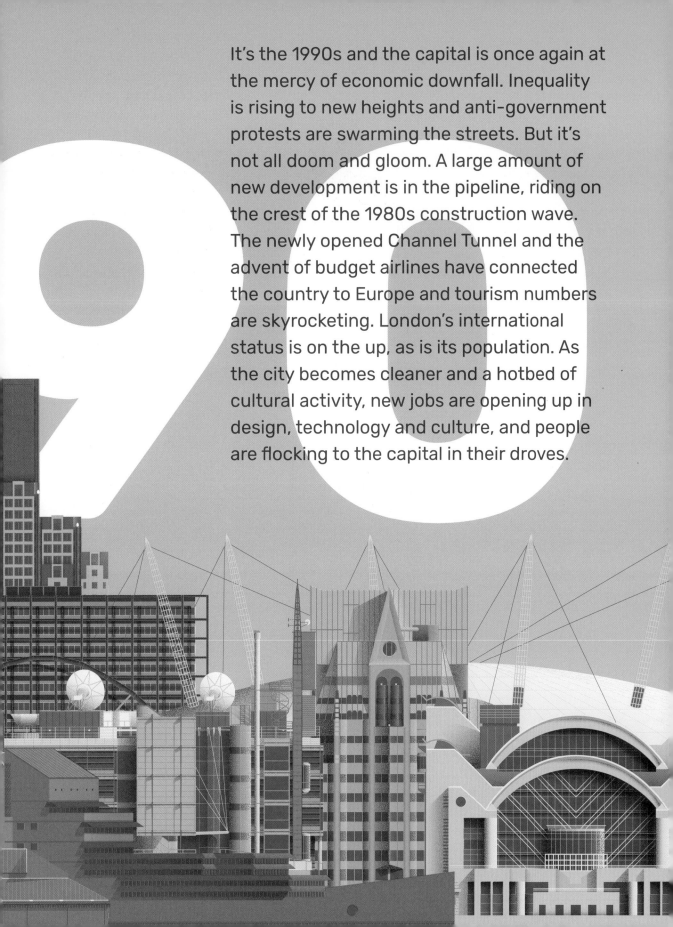

It's the 1990s and the capital is once again at the mercy of economic downfall. Inequality is rising to new heights and anti-government protests are swarming the streets. But it's not all doom and gloom. A large amount of new development is in the pipeline, riding on the crest of the 1980s construction wave. The newly opened Channel Tunnel and the advent of budget airlines have connected the country to Europe and tourism numbers are skyrocketing. London's international status is on the up, as is its population. As the city becomes cleaner and a hotbed of cultural activity, new jobs are opening up in design, technology and culture, and people are flocking to the capital in their droves.

At the beginning of the 1990s, the redevelopment of the Isle of Dogs – in particular Canary Wharf – was in deep trouble. The London Docklands Development Corporation, a government-funded organisation handed the responsibility of renovating the area in the 1980s, had been given unprecedented power in the granting of planning permissions (effectively, they were able to bypass local council rules). This meant that a number of new buildings had been approved without provisions for transport links.

As a result, Canary Wharf had only a few tenants – mainly newspapers from Fleet Street. The Docklands Light Railway eventually opened in 1987, but its capacity was nowhere near the demand. In response to a potential exodus of tenants, the City also relaxed its planning laws in order to grow office space; its central location was still more appealing. This, coupled with global economic recession, meant that the Canadian developer, Olympia & York, soon declared bankruptcy.

One Canada Square
Pelli Clarke Pelli Architects
🕐 1991   📍 E14 5AX   ↕ 235M

Although that's not to say that the site suffered architecturally. **One Canada Square (087)** is the crown jewel of Canary Wharf. Designed by Argentine-American architect César Pelli, who somewhat recycled his earlier '200 Vesey Street' in Manhattan, it became the tallest building in the UK, beating the NatWest Tower (077) after ten years at the top. Even despite it having to be shortened by five floors to accommodate the flight path to the nearby City Airport. Pelli proclaimed that he had built the first skyscraper in London – a claim made many times before.

The skyscraper was nicknamed 'Vertical Fleet Street', as it hosted eight national newspapers, including the Daily Telegraph (004), all of whom had moved here from their traditional home. This big move happened partly because of breaking news, which radically altered the way the newspapers were composed and printed.

The building's stainless-steel façade is nothing if not impressive, but at the time of construction it proved a real nuisance – a side effect of the cladding was that 100,000 people lost their television signal. The case was taken to court and, controversially, the House of Lords concluded that there was no legal right to a good television reception. Fortunately, the BBC built a new relay station to fix the problem.

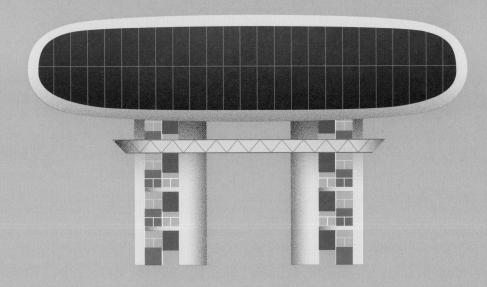

 Lord's Media Centre
Future Systems

🕐 1999   📍 NW8 8QN

Eurocopter AS355

Three new helicopters replaced the police force's Bell 222s, which were more agile and more importantly cheaper to run. But unlike the Bells they weren't capable of instrumental flight and had to be grounded in bad weather. The unit moved to a new home in Fairoaks, Surrey.

From a Canary to a duck – Lord's is very different to Docklands and the architecture it chose was also something completely fresh. **Lord's Media Centre (088)** might be small, but it's one of the most innovative London buildings of the decade. The Lord's Cricket Ground has a tradition of working with leading British architects: in the 1980s, Michael and Patty Hopkins built a new stand using ultra-modern lightweight fabric; a decade later, Nicholas Grimshaw added his high-tech stand.

The new media centre was the first major commission of the visionary Future Systems, and the first aluminium building in the world that used a semi-structural 'skin' – a hybrid of stressed metal held together by aluminium ribs. The novel technology – initially developed for aeronautics – allowed the architects to design a building without any internal clutter, as the load is carried by its 'skin'. It was built in twenty-six sections in shipyards in Rotterdam and Falmouth and assembled on site.

The City was tightly packed by the 1990s, but developers were hungry for more. With the potential competitors at Canary Wharf biting at their heels (although it was still mostly empty at that time), the City planners were open-minded in the proposed exploitation of 'air rights' over railway stations. Previously unseen in London, this trend had its origins in the US and filtered its way across the pond via American architects brought over by overseas investors. Broadgate, a massive development around Liverpool Street Station, was the first to see its application.

Exchange House (089) is one of the most undepreciated buildings in London. It was designed by Skidmore, Owings & Merrill (SOM), as is most of Broadgate. The practice, originally from Chicago, established its first international office in London just after the 'Big Bang', in 1986. Exchange House stands above the tracks of Liverpool Street Station, with very limited space for foundations. SOM solved this with the clever construction of a hybrid bridge building, spanning an incredible seventy-eight metres over the rail tracks.

Two inner archways allow for a column-free interior, while two outer archways show off the construction on the façade and bind the building together. The heavy, industrial-like building seems to levitate, as the open ground floor comprises only a small, circular glass reception area. In 2015, the American Institute of Architects awarded Exchange House the '25-Year Award', given to buildings that have stood the test of time. It was the first time any building in the UK had received the award.

 Exchange House
SOM

🕐 1990   📍 EC2A 2HS

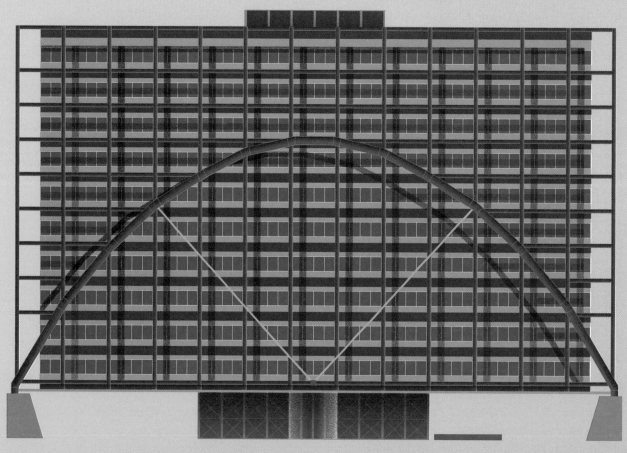

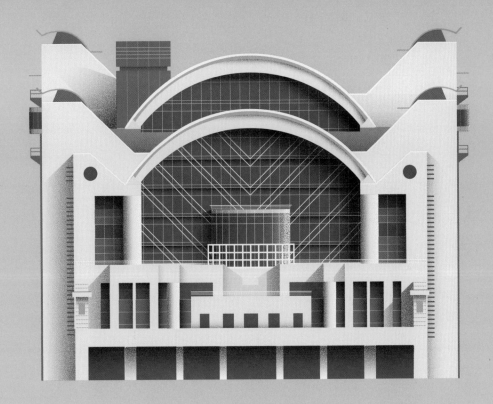

Few architects changed the face of London in recent times as much as Terry Farrell. Born in Sale near Manchester, he was in partnership with Nicholas Grimshaw for fifteen years. When the practice split, Grimshaw continued in his high-tech style, while Farrell pioneered postmodernism in the UK throughout the 1980s. As London grew weary of 'PoMo' after the economic recession, Farrell focused on urbanism and also started working on projects in Hong Kong.

Farrell's **Embankment Place (090)** took on a similar challenge to Exchange House, but on a far larger scale and with a very different result. The building straddles Charing Cross Station, effectively forming its roof. Mindful of its sensitive location on Victoria Embankment, the building steps down towards the River Thames in an attempt to conceal its mass. Huge steel arches take much of the load, also minimising the number of columns piercing the train platform below.

It is the arches that give the building its characteristic profile, reminiscent of the original train station roof. Farrell, not only an architect but also a master urban planner, paid a lot of attention to the streets surrounding the building. He even brought back long lost elements such as railings and lamps, modelled on historic photographs.

 Alban Gate
Farrells

🕐 1992   📍 EC2Y 5AJ

The area surrounding London Wall is one of the earliest inhabited parts of London, and it has seen its fair share of dramatic transformations. During the Blitz, most of the area was reduced to rubble. During the 1950s and 1970s, it saw the construction of a series of modernist office blocks inspired by the architecture of Ludwig Mies van der Rohe. But the area was redeveloped once again in the 1990s, as progress in technology coupled with relaxed planning laws allowed for more floor space.

Standing on the site of the old Roman and medieval gates to the city, **Alban Gate (091)**, also known as 125 London Wall, is a postmodern reinterpretation of a gate house. It's another project that capitalises on air rights, as it straddles a road junction. Two huge towers are connected by a shared core and are set at the same angle as the streets that meet below it.

The building is defined by its engineering, which demands both a minimal footprint and careful spanning of a dual carriageway – no easy feat. By way of credit, the internal bracing is proudly displayed to pedestrians on the open first floor, which connects the building to the Barbican system of walkways (no doubt the proponents of the 'Pedway' system would have been pleased to hear it).

Only few a metres away stands **88 Wood Street (092)**. This became the first City building designed by Richard Rogers after his expensive-to-maintain Lloyd's Building (078). Learning from his mistakes, he chose to tuck most of the expressive details behind glass, safe from the elements and rust. The façade is clad in ultra-transparent frameless glass panels, which affords the workers brilliant views, and also makes the beautiful construction details behind it clearly visible. The glass is specially coated to reduce solar gains and motorised blinds are automatically controlled by photocells measuring the light conditions outside.

These measures improve energy efficiency, although an entirely glass façade is fairly inefficient to begin with. The building utilises deep basements left by the telephone exchange that originally stood on the site. The large air-conditioning units, which usually litter the rooftop, are consequently hidden underground, resulting in an unusually clean roof profile.

(092) **88 Wood Street**
Rogers Stirk Harbour + Partners
🕐 1999   📍 EC2V 7RS   ↕ 75M

Nearby, **200 Aldersgate Tower (093)** closes the west side of the London Wall roundabout. When the building first opened, it was known as Little Britain Tower, named after a local street (not the cult television show). It was first proposed in 1983, but was finished in modified form nine years later. The building consists of more than a dozen towers organised into two wings; this successfully breaks the scale, but makes the interior very hard to navigate.

The wings are connected by a huge glass atrium, spanning twenty-four metres over a busy road. It previously served as a headquarters for a large law firm, but a decade later it made the decision to move to Canary Wharf, looking for a more flexible working space. The building stood empty for years and had to be extensively redesigned and rebranded to attract new tenants.

Eurocopter AS365N Dauphin

The helicopter of the newly established London Air Ambulance carried not only medics, but also senior doctors who helped with pre-hospital care. The service was the first in the world to perform an open-heart surgery on a roadside.

Leyland Olympian

The 1990s saw the privatisation of the London bus service, which was split into a number of smaller companies. Some of them painted their buses in 'untraditional' colours. A new rule was introduced in 1997 specifying that the buses had to be at least 80% red.

 200 Aldersgate Tower
Morey Smith

🕐 1992   📍 EC1A 4HD   ↕ 91M

In concept, the architecture of **Channel 4 (094)**'s building in Victoria is similar to Broadcasting House (011) built sixty years earlier. It's an extended form of public relations and indicates the way the media organisation would like to be viewed. The progressive Channel 4 chose Richard Rogers as the man for the job. He designed the building around a large entrance area, where all the elements meet to impress anyone coming in.

On the right sits an elevator/service tower topped with a transmission mast, while a pile of stacked shipping container-like meeting rooms sits on the left. A concave glass reception forms a link between the dual four-storey office blocks. Later on, this entrance area became even more impressive, with the construction of Channel 4's scaled up three-dimensional logo. The building is clad with grey steel panels, while the exposed frame is exactly the same shade of red as the Golden Gate Bridge in San Francisco – for no apparent reason.

 Channel 4
Rogers Stirk Harbour + Partners

🕐 1994 📍 SW1P 2TX

LTI TX1/4

The long-awaited replacement for the antique FX4 was designed by industrial designer Kenneth Grange. It was produced for twenty years until 2017, with only a few design changes.

Postmodernism, a reaction against mainstream modernism, was eventually absorbed by large architecture practices in this period. But their buildings usually only used the visual elements, missing the witty references and playfulness of the movement's masters. London practice GMW Architects had been building Mies-inspired modernist office blocks for decades, but couldn't resist the new trend.

Its **Minster Court (095)** is a large 'groundscraper', taking up an entire block. However, its separation into three buildings helps to break up the scale and to allow light deeper into the plan. The building was designed in an audacious neo-Gothic fashion, complete with a variety of angles and fins. Dubbed by Londoners 'Munster Court', it got its perfect role in the 1996 film *101 Dalmatians* as the house of Cruella de Vil.

Minster Court
GMW Architects

🕐 1991   📍 EC3R 7DD   ↕ 77M

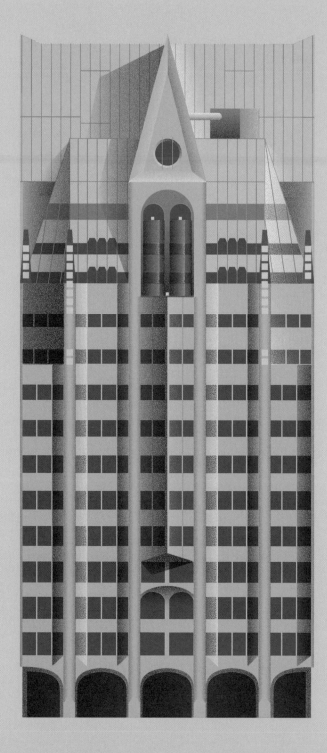

New London Underground Livery

Hailing from New York, graffiti quickly established itself in London and engulfed the underground trains. The unpainted aluminium, which was used by the Underground for fifty-five years, proved impossible to clean and entirely new livery had to be introduced.

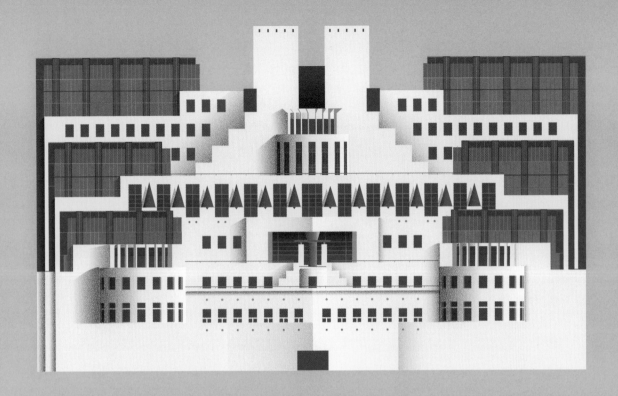

○ **096** **MI6 Building**
Farrells

🕐 1994   📍 SE1 7TP

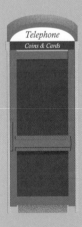

Kiosk KX100+

DCA Design, authors of the minimal and rational design of KX100, 'updated' the phone booth a decade later with a strange plastic dome, referencing the famous K6 kiosk.

The peculiar postmodern design of the **MI6 Building (096)** in Vauxhall is often rationalised as a representation of its secretive tenant. But the reality is that the architect designing the building had no idea who it was for. Terry Farrell had a mere two weeks to deliver a complete design for the headquarters of an unnamed government agency. His studio suspected it might be the Department of Environment and so proposed an alley of trees at the back of the building and bow windows with great river views.

The bomb-proof ziggurat is made out of one-storey-high precast concrete panels assembled on site. The façade incorporates an elaborate system that prevents staining and weathering of the concrete – twenty-four years on, you only have to take one look at the building to know that it works. The windows are triple glazed and (obviously) bullet-proof. In 2000, someone (reportedly the IRA) fired an anti-tank rocket at the building, but it caused only artificial damage. However, twelve years later it was destroyed completely – in the James Bond film *Skyfall*.

The story of **54 Lombard Street (097)** (now 20 Gracechurch) is a case study of change in the City. Barclays Bank had occupied the site since the beginning of the twentieth century. As the bank grew, it bought out surrounding houses and a church, demolished them, and built a large office block in their place during the 1960s. Just twenty years later, the company had outgrown the block and commissioned GMW Architects to design a new building.

The architects completely redeveloped the site, and the new postmodern complex opened in 1994. It comprises three rounded top towers, which in a way resemble the Chrysler Building in New York City, although without its crown.

The City planners allowed the building to stretch surprisingly high in a bid to prevent the decamping of the bank to London Docklands. The strategy was successful for a short time, but only seven years later the bank announced its move to Canary Wharf.

Jubilee Line Extension

The much-anticipated connection between Canary Wharf and central London was finally opened in the last days of 1999. The Dockland's developers initially promised to cover the cost, but in the end they contributed only 5%.

(097) **54 Lombard Street**
GMW Architects

🕐 1994 📍 EC3V 9DH ↕ 87M

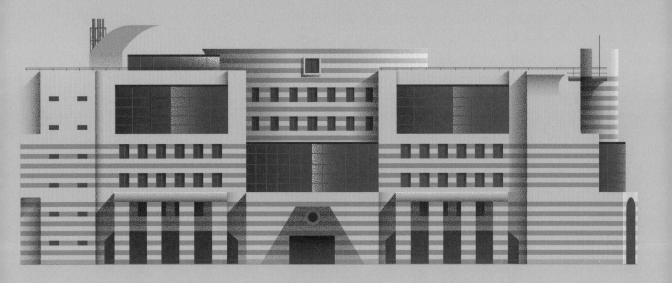

(098) **No 1 Poultry**
James Stirling

🕐 1997   📍 EC2R 8EJ

The site of **No 1 Poultry (098)** saw possibly the longest planning process in London's history. It began in 1958, when Rudolph Palumbo started buying properties in the area, which is surrounded by various masterpieces of the great English architects. Rudolph's son Peter Palumbo commissioned one of the most influential architects of the century, German architect Ludwig Mies van der Rohe, to replace the existing Victorian buildings. Mies designed a nineteen-storey bronze-clad tower and a new public space.

Mies died just a few months later, which meant he was spared witness to the bitter battle between planners and developers that his design unleashed. Two long decades of outrage, reviews and public inquiry – due to the proposed removal of some listed buildings – resulted in the eventual rejection of the development. By that point, modernism was seen as outdated. The developer commissioned Glasgow-born James Stirling, a key figure in postmodern architecture, to draught a more up-to-date design.

Ironically, the 1985 design was not completed until 1997, five years after Stirling's death. (One might say the project was cursed.) By then, trends had evolved, and the building was deemed a ghost from the past. Stirling's ballsy building proved to be as controversial as the original Mies proposal, although it respects and references the surrounding buildings (even if it doesn't appear to at first glance). In 2016, the building became the youngest listed building in the UK, billed as an 'unsurpassed example of commercial postmodernism'.

The 1990s also saw the rise of grand cultural structures. Two of the most talked about were The British Library and the Millennium Dome. **The British Library (099)**, the UK's largest public building of the century, opened in 1997. It took a staggering thirty-six years to take the project from inception to opening, largely due to government meddling. Today, the library remains one of the largest in the world – a little hard to believe on first sight. The huge structure is an iceberg of sorts, reaching thirty metres down by way of five underground floors.

Its architect, Colin St John Wilson, put considerable effort into softening the giant scale. The façade is clad in the same Leicester brick as the neighbouring St Pancras Station and the building's profile is gradually stepped down. However, these measures did little to stop crude comments from the press, Prince Charles (as ever) and Parliament. Wilson's career was over before the Queen cut the ribbon. He dissolved his partnership and went to work at his wife's practice. Since then, the library received Grade I listing and made it into a small club of exceptional buildings.

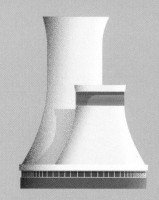

Blackwall Tunnel Ventilation Shaft

Terry Farrell's design from 1967 was inspired by Oscar Niemeyer's work at Brasilia. It is now safely enveloped by the Millennium Dome.

British Aerospace 146

The most successful and probably the last British civil jet airliner was designed for an extremely short landing and take-off. This made it ideal for the small London City Airport. A variant of it still operates from the airport.

(099) The British Library
Colin St John Wilson

🕐 1998   📍 NW1 2DB

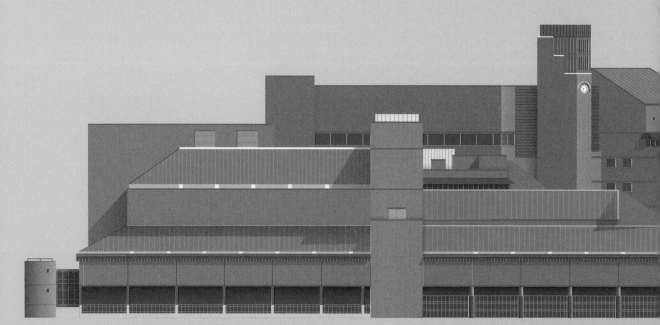

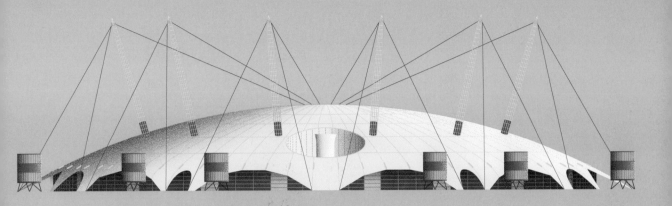

(100) Millennium Dome
Richard Rogers & Mike Davies
🕐 1999   📍 SE10 0DX

Over in London Docklands, the **Millennium Dome (100)** was developed to host the 'Millennium Experience' – a cultural programme intended to attract people from all around the country. It was an utter failure, as the project ran out of money only four weeks after opening. Hundreds of millions of pounds disappeared and the media had a field day, largely blaming the architect, Richard Rogers.

But the flop wasn't caused by the architecture, far from it. The innovative and cost-friendly building comprised barely 7% of the total budget. The rest – 93% – was spent on the programme, fees, marketing and other amenities, although it's hard to believe. Originally intended as a revival of the successful Festival of Britain of 1951 (see p.42), the dome became one of the biggest political embarrassments of recent history. Rogers' architecture was unfairly overshadowed by the controversy.

He had designed the largest dome and the largest single-roofed structure in the world, and under budget. The glass fibre roof is supported by twelve bright yellow masts that echo the structure of Skylon (038). Seventy kilometres of cables keep the roof in place. Interestingly, the dome features a large circular cut-out on the southwestern side, a result of the Blackwall Tunnel ventilation shafts. The concrete shafts were designed by Terry Farrell in the 1960s and listed in 2000, meaning the dome had to be designed around them. Following the failure of the Millennium Experience, the dome was sold – reportedly for £1 – and is now more commonly known as the O2 Arena. In 2012, after selling 2 million tickets, it topped the world's list of most popular entertainment venues. A happy ending to an otherwise sombre tale.

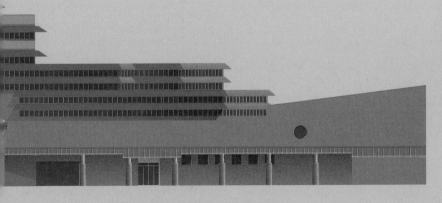

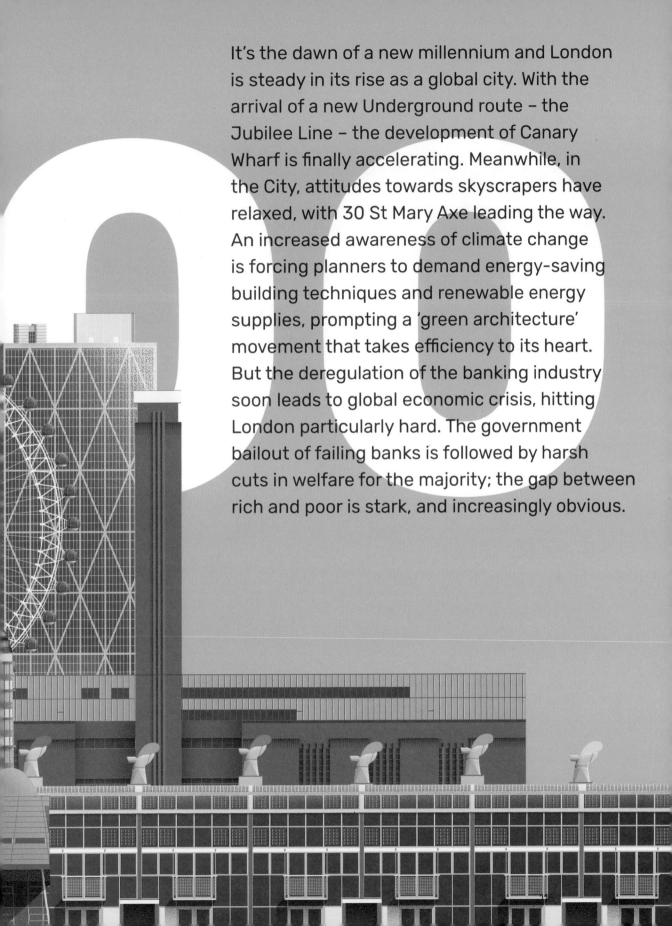

It's the dawn of a new millennium and London is steady in its rise as a global city. With the arrival of a new Underground route – the Jubilee Line – the development of Canary Wharf is finally accelerating. Meanwhile, in the City, attitudes towards skyscrapers have relaxed, with 30 St Mary Axe leading the way. An increased awareness of climate change is forcing planners to demand energy-saving building techniques and renewable energy supplies, prompting a 'green architecture' movement that takes efficiency to its heart. But the deregulation of the banking industry soon leads to global economic crisis, hitting London particularly hard. The government bailout of failing banks is followed by harsh cuts in welfare for the majority; the gap between rich and poor is stark, and increasingly obvious.

 101 **Portcullis House**
Hopkins Architects

🕐 2001 📍 SW1A 2JR

Parliament Emblem

The portcullis has a historic connection with the Houses of Parliament, and aside from giving its name to the new building, it is also used as the Parliament's emblem.

Portcullis House (101) in Westminster is an offshoot of the Palace of Westminster, the home of the British government. Since the palace is a protected UNESCO World Heritage Site, the extension had to keep its distance and so was built across the street. It hosts offices and facilities for more than 200 members of parliament, and is connected to the palace by an underground tunnel – so employees don't have to run across the busy road above. Hopkins Architects designed a building that is traditional in concept, but uses the latest materials and technology.

It forms a classical square block with a protected courtyard in the middle. The bomb-proof building features steep sloping roofs and tall chimney structures (part of a system of natural ventilation), creating a profile not dissimilar to its centuries-old neighbour. Part of the development was the new Westminster Underground Station, which was built seven floors below ground – the deepest excavation ever made in central London. The foundations of the nearby Big Ben had to be strengthened, but it still moved a couple of centimetres as a result.

City Hall (102) – rather harshly nicknamed the Glass Testicle – is home to the relaunched and rebranded London Council. Now named the Greater London Authority (GLA), the organisation is smarter, smaller and more streamlined – much like the building itself. Perhaps symbolically, the structure is privately owned and only rented by the GLA, marking a new era of outsourcing and the much more limited power of the council – once the biggest landlord in the world, with the largest architecture department on the planet.

City Hall was designed by Ken Shuttleworth of Foster + Partners, and centred on the idea of a 'non-polluting' public building. Computer modelling – brand new technology at the time – enabled architects to shape buildings into previously impossible forms. But City Hall's shape wasn't designed just for show. It minimises areas exposed to the sun; as is the case with most glass office buildings, too much direct sunlight creates excessive levels of heat and the subsequent need for energy hungry air conditioning units. To combat the issue further, cold groundwater is pumped around the building to cool it down.

All of this worked on paper, but unfortunately the reality proved different. Disappointingly, the building has only an Energy Performance Certificate rating of 'D' ('A' is the best and 'G' the worst), the same as Portcullis House (101). This is due in part to the rise in the number of people working inside, an inevitable outcome of the growing council. Building managers also had to figure out how to use the system properly, which proved time consuming. The impressive staircase, spiralling 500 metres through the building, is reminiscent of Foster + Partner's parallel work – the Reichstag in Berlin, where people can see the government at work from a similar ramp. Unfortunately, the ramp is closed to the public most of the time due to security concerns.

(102) **City Hall**
Foster + Partners
🕐 2002 📍 SE1 2AA

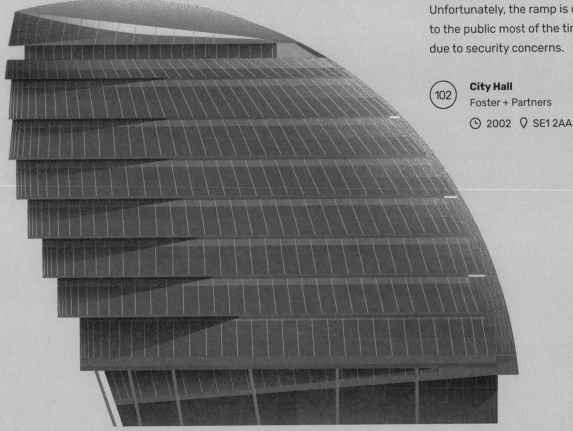

MD900 Explorer

The new helicopter of the Whitechapel-based London Air Ambulance doesn't use a tail rotor, which helps it to land in the crowded streets of the capital. A second machine was bought with the help of charity donations in 2015.

Before **Tate Modern (103)** became one of the 'coolest art galleries in the world', it was warming up the atmosphere as Bankside Power Station (053). The large complex closed its gates in 1981, after high oil prices made it too expensive to run. The power station stood empty for thirteen long years before the Tate Gallery announced its plans to turn the space into a new art museum. Swiss architects Herzog and de Meuron were tasked with giving the building a new lease of life.

Instead of large design gestures, which one would expect from a modern art gallery, their work largely consisted of clearing up the structure and adding some modest additions. At the heart of the gallery stands the Turbine Hall, a breath-taking space of giant proportions that is regularly filled with similarly sized art commissions. The huge visitor numbers soon proved lifts and facilities too small, and so the gallery began plans for an extension (119).

 103 **Tate Modern**
Herzog and de Meuron
🕐 2000   📍 SE1 9TG

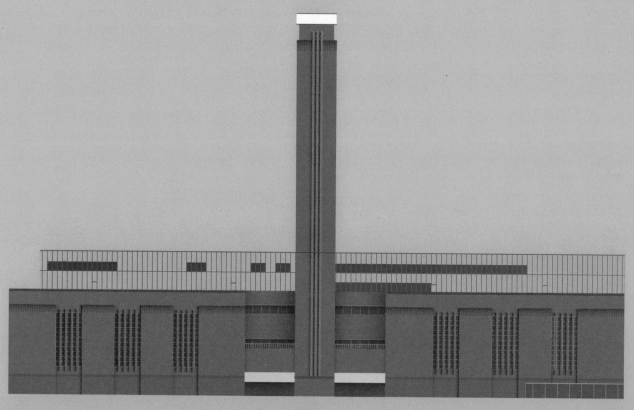

**Mercedes-Benz O530G
'Bendy Bus' Citaro**

These high-capacity articulated buses were introduced in 2002. Their three doors sped up boarding, but gave them the nickname the 'free bus', as many people didn't bother to tap their Oyster cards once on board. The buses also proved dangerous to cyclists and Boris Johnson promised their replacement as part of his mayor campaign. He succeeded.

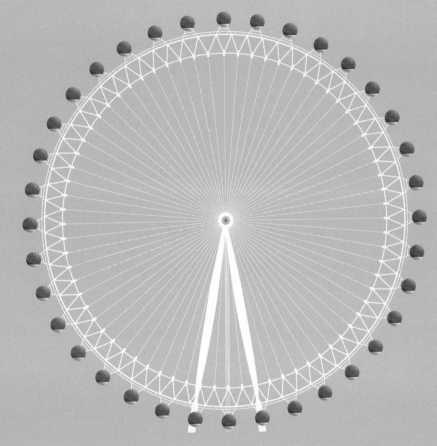

 London Eye
Julia Barfield and David Marks

🕐 2000 📍 SE1 7PB ↕ 158M

The **London Eye (104)**, originally called the Millennium Wheel, was one of the so-called 'Millennium Projects' that sprung up at the end of the twentieth century (see Millennium Dome (100)). The initial idea was formed in 1993, but construction didn't start until January 1999. The opening was scheduled for New Year's Eve, and so construction became a race against time.

Snapped cables, occupation by protesters and unusually high tides, which left no space for barges to pass under the bridges, all caused delays. All hope for completing on time was lost just one day before the celebrations, when one of the thirty-two pods failed a safety check. The opening had to be postponed until March 2000, but it was all worth it in the end. Incredibly, 6 million people took it for a spin in the first six months alone, breaking all predictions.

The architects, husband and wife team David Marks and Julia Barfield, originally received permission for a structure lasting only five years, after which it would have to be taken down. But its unexpected success means the wheel is now embedded in the London skyline, even making it onto seat covers (moquettes) on the Underground. Copycat designs have seen Ferris wheels pop up in cities all around the world.

Norman Foster is one of the few living architects to have become a household name. His buildings, many of which were produced in this period, have helped shape London as a modern metropolis. He had a modest upbringing in industrial Manchester, where he started working as a clerk at the town hall aged just sixteen. After undertaking national service with the RAF, he decided to study architecture at Manchester University. A model student, he won a fellowship at the Yale School of Architecture in the US. There he met Richard Rogers – they later formed Team 4 together with Wendy Chessman and Su Brumwell. The small but influential partnership lasted a couple of years, but later split into the separate Foster and Rogers practices we all know today.

HSBC Tower (105), also known as 8 Canada Square, is a showcase of a new generation of office buildings, and arguably the reason why Canary Wharf (after all those years) became so attractive to giant business corporations. Foster had designed the bank's monumental (and expensive) Hong Kong headquarters in the 1980s – this time he was tasked with creating a cheaper and more easily adaptable structure. A new system of construction, which came on the sails of American investors flocking to the City after the Big Bang, dictated that the architect design only the shell and core of the building.

Tenants were then free to fit it out for use as required.
The role of Foster + Partners was in some ways very limited. The sleek tower, softened by rounded corners, is as flexible (or without character) as possible. Just unpeel the bank's logo on the top and someone else is free to move in. The tower is flanked by two siblings – 33 Canada Square and One Canada Square (087). Both have exactly the same floor space and height (if you dismiss the pyramid on the latter). This shows the difference between Canary Wharf and the City, where every site is in the latter distinctive and has its own characteristic requirements. HSBC sold the building just four years after moving in, then bought it again five years later, only to sell it once more. This shrewd property juggling resulted in huge profits for the bank.

Eurocopter EC145

These Metropolitan Police helicopters hovering over London are now as common as pigeons. Equipped with night vision and heat cameras, they operate twenty-four hours a day.

  HSBC Tower
Foster + Partners

🕐 2002 📍 E14 5HQ ↕ 200M

30 St Mary Axe (106), better known as the Gherkin, is without a doubt the most recognisable twenty-first-century building in London. Its story is long and painful, although not without a happy ending. It started with a terrorist attack in 1993, when the IRA set off a truck bomb in the heart of the City. Many buildings were damaged, including the NatWest Tower (077). But the listed Baltic Exchange was hardest hit and was put up for redevelopment. Foster produced a design for a 386-metre-tall Millennium Tower, but it was way too high (the Shard (117) is seventy metres lower) and was rejected by planners. In response, Foster's practice developed a new, organically shaped and much shorter design, in cooperation with the city planners. Surprisingly, the planners recommended building higher than originally intended, to improve the building's proportions.

The tower is wrapped in an elegant diagonal steel structure, which removes the need for any internal supports. The structure rotates by five degrees on every floor, creating an elegant façade with a twist. The Gherkin quickly gained global notoriety and often appears in 'establishing shots' of London-based films – something many architects dream of (although perhaps not the architects of Thamesmead, after Kubrick's *A Clockwork Orange*). Similarly to City Hall (102), the Gherkin was (and still is) promoted as a triumph of green, sustainable architecture. But the complex system of natural ventilation that was supposed to cut the energy consumption was abandoned when it became clear the tenants preferred machine air conditioning. On top of that, one of its architects, Ken Shuttleworth, turned against it just a few years later, noting that the fully glazed façade is expensive and plays havoc with interior temperature control.

Thames Clippers

With its roads jam-packed, London looked back on its natural artery, the River Thames. New lines of fast boats now ferry commuters from suburbs on the river to the city centre.

(106) **30 St Mary Axe**
Foster + Partners

🕐 2004 📍 EC3A 8BF ↕ 180M

The increasing number of towers springing up in London during this period might suggest that all height restrictions had been forgotten, but the case of **Broadgate Tower (107)** reminds us that this wasn't the case. The law protecting views of St Paul's Cathedral from certain areas was still in place, most notably in the preservation of the sight-line from King Henry's Mound in Richmond Park, nearly ten miles away. This visual corridor doesn't end at the cathedral, but continues for another mile and a half behind it and so falls directly over a part of the Broadgate site. This limited the maximum height of the development. Instead of designing one large, low building, the Chicago office of SOM decided to split the site in two. A skyscraper, tucked into the 'unprotected' corner of the site, is joined by a lower building on the other side. The tower hovers above a busy railway track, as does the nearby Exchange House (089). It adopts the same bridge structure for spanning the railway, but in a less apparent fashion.

Structural steel supports criss-cross the façade, holding the building together, and at the base a giant steel A-frame distributes the loads. The frame also creates an outside area that links the two buildings together. Being right on the border of the City and Shoreditch, it initiated an 'overspill' of office buildings from the City into the surrounding areas, which are slowly being consumed block by block.

 107 **Broadgate Tower**
SOM

🕐 2009 📍 EC2A 2EW ↕ 161M

LIBRARY

From bartering to books. **Peckham Library (108)** was part of an ambitious regeneration plan for Peckham, one of the most deprived areas in the city. Northampton-born Will Alsop designed a bold, colourful building that sees the main library space hover above a paved square below, supported by thin columns at varied angles. The decision to elevate the reading rooms (the ground and first floors consist of information and media centres) makes sense once you glimpse the incredible view of London's skyline. Two 'pods' that act as conference rooms break up the main space as well as the roof line, which is also adorned with a bright orange 'tongue' that shades a dramatic skylight. For anyone confused as to the building's purpose, a large sign in friendly rounded letters confirms the site's literary credentials.

The design proved to be flexible, too, as parts of the interior had to be rebuilt for changing needs. The original natural ventilation wasn't enough, as crowds filled the space, and so air conditioning had to be installed. The system didn't fit in the building itself, and now sits behind it. The new library was a huge success. Its membership skyrocketed and it became especially popular with teenagers – the number of fifteen- to nineteen-year-olds going to the library is twice the average in the borough. Seemingly an impossible brief, calling for a prestigious (but not elitist) building that would attract hard-to-impress young readers, was met. Since then, Southwark Council has built two more brand new libraries in Canada Water, designed by CZWG, and Camberwell.

 Peckham Library
Will Alsop & Christophe Egret

🕐 2000 📍 SE15 5JR

Sikorsky S-76C++

The official helicopter of the queen and the royal family was upgraded in 2009. It's unclear whether Prince Harry or Prince William, both pilots themselves, are allowed behind the controls.

Legible London

A city-wide wayfinding system featuring local maps and travel information was introduced in 2008. Hugely successful, it helps both tourists and locals navigate London's twisting streets.

New art galleries were popping up, too. **Rivington Place (109)** was the first gallery to be backed by public funding for forty years. Shoreditch had recently become popular with the creative industry thanks to a large number of empty warehouses with (initially) low rents. Among these trendy new studios, Ghanaian-British architect David Adjaye designed a low-key yet impressive art space. Its dark frontage (Adjaye's trademark) represents a clever play on perspective. The tight location means that viewers can only really see the building only from one angle, and so Adjaye has made it count.

The grid of windows and panels grows wider with distance, creating an optical illusion whereby the building appears much shorter than it is. The zig-zag roof structure – a nod to the surrounding factory skylights – uses the same trick, stretching with distance. In addition, there are more rows of windows than actual floors, making the building seem taller. In many cases, the interior rooms have two levels of window – the bottom row offering a street view and the top a nod to the sky.

 Rivington Place
David Adjaye

🕐 2007 📍 EC2A 3BA

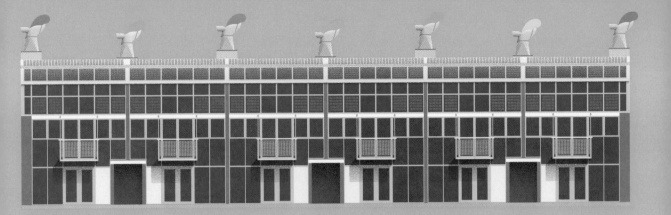

The trend for 'green' architecture came to influence not only office architecture, but also new housing. **BedZED (110)** is an experimental ecological housing development built on the southern outskirts of London, near Croydon. The whole structure was planned with the aim of limiting the carbon footprint of the buildings. Materials, many of them reclaimed, were sourced from as close as possible to the site, in order to limit transport emissions. The flats have glazed conservatories to the south, which capture solar energy, while the coldest north side has only small windows to reduce loss of heat. Other energy solutions include green roofs, thick insulated walls and natural ventilation systems. As a result, the flats use only 40% of the energy required by a typical family home. Proof that it is possible to design sustainable housing without creating something resembling a Hobbit village.

Much of London's drive to become more eco-friendly was kickstarted under Ken Livingstone, who became the first London mayor after the position was established alongside the GLA in 2000 (see p.117). In the 1980s, he had been the leader of the Greater London Council, before it was abolished by Margaret Thatcher's government. His controversial socialist policies earned him the nickname Red Ken, although as mayor, he was supportive of business and waved through large commercial developments. He greatly improved the London bus network, but his most important legacy is arguably the introduction of the Congestion Charge – an automatic system that charges vehicles driving into central London. Although watered down by Livingstone's successor Boris Johnson, it still helps to reduce unnecessary car journeys.

 BedZED
Bill Dunster
🕐 2002 📍 CR4 4HS

Congestion Charge

From 2003, drivers accessing much of central London were required to pay a fee. The system is automatic as traffic cameras scan car registration numbers.

London's streets, clouded in record-breaking toxic pollution, are changing dramatically once more. New cycle paths criss-cross the city, a number of electric buses are on the roads and black cabs are slowly following suit. New buildings are now more efficient and low-energy consumption has become a (sometimes overblown) sales point. But it's not all rosy. Councils and building companies are failing to provide enough homes for a growing population. And yet London's skyline is changing faster than ever amid skyscraper madness – towers are appearing everywhere, even in boroughs previously untouched by high-rises.

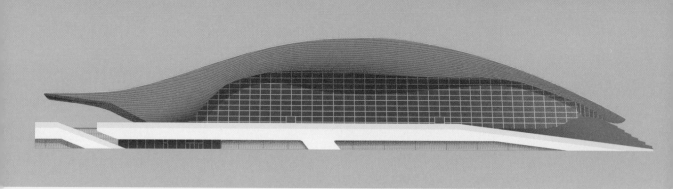

Preparations for the 2012 Olympic Games in London were hugely affected by the unfolding financial crisis. The previous summer Olympic Games in Beijing had been the most expensive so far, as China wanted to prove itself as a global power. Britain's winning bid in 2005 for the 2012 games was rather more modest, but even that budget was to prove too grand when the crisis hit. A revamped plan was set in motion to deliver a sustainable and affordable games. Post-industrial zones of the Lee Valley in east London were transformed into an impressive Olympic Park, designed to require minimal maintenance. 98% of building waste from the demolished factories on the site was reused or recycled.

With a 'legacy' in mind, stadiums for less popular sports were only temporary structures, since they wouldn't attract enough users after the Games.

Thankfully, a reduced budget didn't stand in the way of good architecture. Zaha Hadid's design for the **Aquatics Centre (111)** was chosen via an international competition, long before the decision to make the Games more sustainable and economically viable – the original design had to be scaled down and compromised to reduce the cost, although the building still cost three-and-half times the intended budget. The main feature of the stadium is an elegant, wave-inspired roof, typical of Hadid's work.

But what seems so natural and light is held together only thanks to an extremely complex roof structure that is twelve metres thick at some points. The engineers from Arup probably had nightmares about it long after they finished the work.

The venue had to be built with a large enough seating capacity to accommodate the Olympic crowds, but also to account for the fact that they would struggle to fill seats once the Games were over. A clever solution came in the form of two temporary wings, with a total of 15,000 seats, that were built alongside the stadium. The wings were later removed and the sides closed off with a glazed façade; the capacity is now just 2,500 seats.

Aquatics Centre
Zaha Hadid Architects

🕐 2011 📍 E20 2ZQ

ArcelorMittal Orbit Tower
Anish Kapoor & Cecil Balmond

🕐 2014 📍 E20 2AD ↕ 114M

The Velodrome (112), built at the other end of the Olympic Park, is a work by Hopkins Architects. They had the perfect advisor in British track cyclist Chris Hoy, who won three gold medals in Beijing (and a further two in the Velodrome). The simplest way to describe the stadium's shape is to use its nickname, The Pringle (a favourite crisp snack in the UK). Unlike the Aquatic Centre, the building's form is a result of a pragmatic merging of engineering and design. The roof, ten times lighter than Hadid's, is made from a net of thirty-six-millimetre-thick cables. The cables are set in a grid pattern and covered with timber and waterproof membrane. The efficient building exceeded requirements for sustainability and was delivered ahead of schedule and on budget.

The beautifully landscaped Olympic Park, which can retain water in the case of floods, is spoiled by the glowingly red **ArcelorMittal Orbit Tower (113)**. The strange structure wasn't in the masterplan at all, but was pushed through by the then mayor, Boris Johnson. It didn't matter that it contradicted the London Games' ethos of austerity and sustainability – Johnson claimed that the Olympic area needed 'something extra', and chose a design for a huge sculpture (complete with a spiral walkway and public viewing platform) by artist Anish Kapoor and engineer Cecil Balmond. Perhaps the only positive thing about this tower-sculpture is that it was largely paid for by Indian steel magnate Lakshmi Mittal and not by British taxpayers.

The Velodrome
Hopkins Architects

🕐 2011 📍 E20 3AB

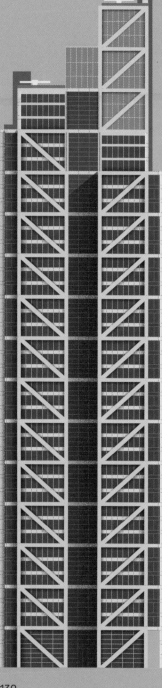

Boris Johnson was London mayor between 2008 and 2016. Originally a political journalist, he was very keen to leave his mark on the capital. A cyclist himself, he helped to improve cycling safety and supported the building of numerous new cycle paths. That said, the system of hire bicycles is unfairly nicknamed 'Boris Bikes', as it is technically Livingstone's work. Unfortunately, many of Johnson's other projects were megalomaniac and ended with mixed results. The unnecessary ArcelorMittal Orbit Tower (see previous page), the pointless cable car over the River Thames and the impractical (but beautiful – a Thomas Heatherwick design) new Routemaster bus all share Johnson's lack of attention to detail.

In central London, a new generation of skyscrapers, slowed down by the 2008 economic crash, arrived. **Heron Tower (114)** was originally designed in 1999, before the Gherkin (106) arrived and demonstrated the plausibility of skyscrapers in the City. It took years to get planning approval, mainly because of its proximity to St Paul's Cathedral when viewed from Waterloo Bridge. The top of the tower was remodelled and approved, and the project was finally finished in 2011.

It became the tallest skyscraper in the City, beating NatWest Tower (077) after an incredible thirty-one years at the top. The speculative development is made of two stacks of three-storey units, which are apparently an ideal size for letting. Seen from the north, these units are clearly distinguishable thanks to the structural bracing that frames each one of them. Unfortunately, the views from the other sides are less interesting.

Elizabeth Line

Originally known as Crossrail, this is one of the largest construction projects in Europe – a sixty-mile-long railway connecting London with western and eastern commuter towns.

Boris Bike

London mayor Ken Livingstone was so impressed with the bicycle rental system in Paris that he decided to copy the idea. It finally launched in 2010, when Boris Johnson was mayor, hence the unfair nickname.

(114) **Heron Tower**
Paul Simovic,
Gene Kohn, Dennis Hill

🕐 2011 📍 EC2N 4AY ↕ 230M

Unusually, the core – incorporating the lifts and services – is not positioned in the middle of the structure, but along the southern edge. This solution helps to keep the office layout clear and uninterrupted. The core also shades most of the sunlight, often a problem for a fully glazed building, and so helps to reduce the use of air conditioning and electricity. Also helping out with the energy bill are 48,000 solar cells scattered around the southern façade. These were added to satisfy the London Plan's requirements to derive a portion of the building's energy from renewable sources.

The financial crisis led to the cancellation of a number of large projects, but most of them were simply delayed. Graham Stirk of Rogers Stirk Harbour + Partners (Richard Rogers renamed what had been Richard Rogers and Partners to demonstrate the importance of his partner architects) first sketched the **Leadenhall Building (115)** in 2001. A long fourteen years later, it finally opened. By then, it had already become known as the Cheesegrater. Like any other skyscraper in London, it was put under heavy scrutiny over its height and its potential for 'spoiling views'. Seen from Fleet Street, the building had to lean away from St Paul's in order to allow space for the view.

The outcome worked to the designer's advantage, resulting in a very distinctive profile. The elegant shape, efficient engineering and superb construction details made the Cheesegrater one of the best new skyscrapers in London. Across the road stands the Lloyd's Building (078), which the same practice had completed three decades earlier. The two buildings together show just how much architecture and the City had progressed during the intervening years. And although very different, both buildings carry a specific 'house style' – something few architecture companies ever achieve.

Wrightbus Routemaster

The brainchild of Boris Johnson, who wanted to bring back the Routemaster bus. The hybrid bus was designed by Thomas Heatherwick in a hasty process that led to a host of technical problems. The main feature, an open back platform that has to be manned, was abandoned for the same reason discovered forty years previously – it was expensive to have an additional member of staff at the back of the bus.

 Leadenhall Building
Rogers Stirk Harbour + Partners
⏱ 2015 📍 EC3V 4AB ↕ 225M

CS3

Cycle Superhighway

Protected cycle paths leading from suburbs to the centre of London are slowly being introduced, giving commuters a healthy alternative. Over half of all the traffic on Victoria Embankment during peak commuting hours is now cyclists.

20 Fenchurch Street (116) was suitably nicknamed the Walkie Talkie due to its complicated shape; it certainly feels more like product design than architecture. The building, designed by Uruguayan Rafael Viñoly, got an unusual amount of press coverage, but for all the wrong reasons. As with other big (and problematic) developments, it had to 'give something back' in order to be approved by planners in the City.

An impressive garden/observation deck accessible to the public (if you book three days in advance) did the job. In order to maximise the size of the most profitable floors with a river view, the building swells towards the top. This gives the skyscraper a rather unflattering, top-heavy profile. Its neighbours had to be paid off, to give up their right to light (see Broadcasting House (011)).

But what really damaged the building's reputation was the 'death ray' created by its concaved south façade. The concentrated reflection of the sun's rays was so powerful that it melted plastic parts of a car parked nearby. This was a recurring nightmare for Viñoly apparently – his earlier Vdara Hotel in Las Vegas had the same problem. The skyscraper, re-christened Walkie Scorchie, was later fixed with the installation of fins, which redirected the sun's rays. The building went on to win the Carbuncle cup – an award for the ugliest building in the UK. However, the accolade did little to deter a Hong Kong buyer, who paid a record £1.3 billion for the building in 2017.

Charging Point

Hundreds of chargers for electric vehicles are popping up around London in a rush to upgrade the infrastructure for the twenty-first century.

 20 Fenchurch Street
Rafael Viñoly

🕐 2014   📍 EC3M 8AF   ↕ 160M

What happens when British developers team up with an Italian architect, Qatari investors and a Hong Kong hotel? **The Shard (117)** happens. At 310 metres, it became the tallest building in the European Union, although globally it's not even in the top hundred – Europe never played that game anyway. The Shard stands over a major transport hub, London Bridge Station, and offers spectacular views of the financial district across the river. Its location, away from the two main clusters of skyscrapers, paradoxically helped it rise higher. Unlike in many cases in the City, no protected view corridors limit the site and, it's not in the landing path of aeroplanes as is Canary Wharf.

The design sees an elongated pyramid gradually break up towards the top. It's a shame that the ground level is so underwhelming. As the style of this decade dictates, the tower is completely glazed. To reduce heat gain from the sun, the façade has two skins with a ventilated space between them, and automatically operated shades are of course a must. Still, the building is an energy hog. The lower floors are dedicated to offices, a luxury hotel occupies the middle space, and flats for the super-rich occupy the highest floors. The top floor contains a fairly expensively ticketed viewing platform accessible to the public. All ten ultra-luxury flats on top of the tower remain unsold, more than five years after opening.

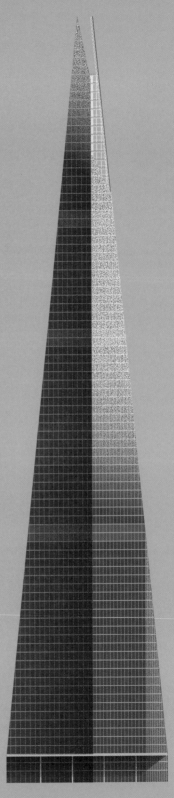

The Shard
Renzo Piano Building Workshop
🕐 2012　♀ SE1 9SG　↕ 310M

 Central St Giles Court
Renzo Piano Building Workshop
🕐 2010   📍 WC2H 8AG

In the twelve years that it took to design and build The Shard (117), the architect Renzo Piano contributed another building to London's skyline. Born in Genoa, Piano became an architect of international renown, although his main office is still based in his home town. Early in his career, Piano formed a practice with Richard Rogers. Practically unknown and with not much experience, they went on to win the competition for the Centre Georges Pompidou in Paris, beating architecture giants such as Oscar Niemeyer and Philip Johnson. Their unconventional design was extremely challenging, and when the building was finished six years later, Piano and Rogers went their separate ways.

The building almost broke them, but it certainly put them on the map. **Central St Giles Court (118)** was built on an 'island' surrounded by busy roads, previously occupied by a 1950s office building. The architect introduced new pathways leading through the site, offering shortcuts to passers-by. The massive bulk of the new development is skilfully modelled by Piano, who employs every trick in the book to break it down to a scale more appropriate to the area. Blocks vary in height, the top floors are recessed and the façades form a rainbow of vivid colours.

The terracotta tiles were originally made in Germany before being assembled into blocks in Poland and sent on to Camden for installation. It's amazing how much of an international process construction has become, but it is similarly troubling – the CO_2 emissions linked to these materials and their transportation must have been significant. See BedZED (110) for a more environmentally friendly approach to construction.

Aeryon SkyRanger

The Metropolitan Police Service is now trialling drones for a wide range of uses: from chasing moped gangs to searching for cannabis farms. Its price is a fraction of the operating costs of a helicopter, but one might argue that it's uncomfortably dystopian.

A victim of its own success perhaps, Tate Modern (103) was in need of more space practically immediately after opening. A solution was found in the form of the handsome **Blavatnik Building (119)**. Herzog and de Meuron, architects of the original conversion, were called up again. The modesty of the original refurbishment was abandoned and they designed a bold and confident ziggurat to adjoin the original building. An initial proposal saw the building fully glazed, but after strong criticism from the public it was (thankfully) redesigned and now incorporates beautiful brickwork. The interior is finished in rather rough but suitably minimal bare concrete and wood.

And in order not to repeat previous mistakes, the new building includes an excessive number of elevators (whether this really helps is questionable; it's impossible to catch a lift that doesn't stop at every single floor!). One of its greatest features is a viewing platform on top of the building, which is, like the museum, free of charge. However, the neighbours may think otherwise – the owners of the flats in the expensive (and glass-walled) apartment blocks across the road have repeatedly tried to prevent nosy tourists peering into their million-pound pads.

 119   **Blavatnik Building**
Herzog and de Meuron

🕐 2016   📍 SE1 9TG

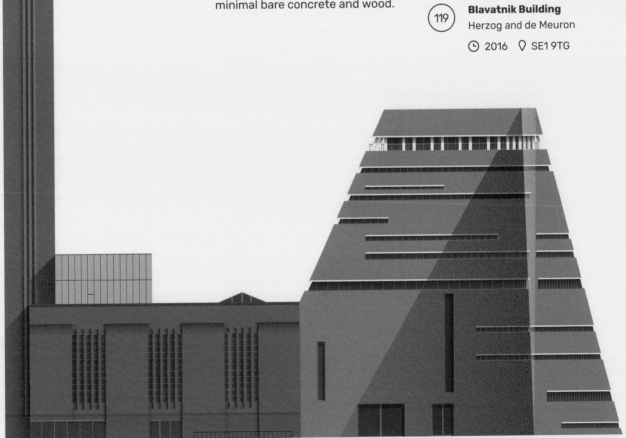

The economic crisis prompted only a momentary pause in the development of luxury flats. London, with its stable political position and rising property values, became a favourite investment spot for the global rich. A group that, according to Transparency International, included corrupt individuals looking to launder their money while enjoying a luxury lifestyle. Developers chasing high profits focused on delivering structures suitable for these big-spending clients. This, coupled with staggeringly high land values, raised property prices to levels altogether unreachable by the vast majority of locals. It remains London's biggest headache.

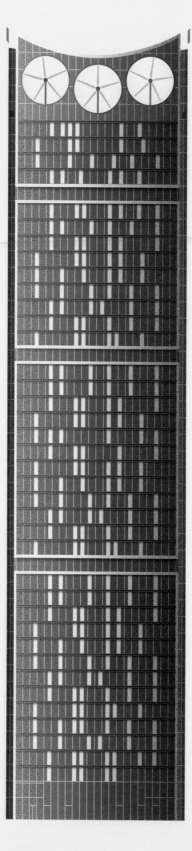

Strata SE1 (120) was the first step in yet another regeneration of Elephant & Castle (see p.64). The area, as with most of Southwark, has seen much controversial replacement of council housing by new flashy developments. The 148-metre-tall 'Electric Razor' was the first building in the world designed with integral wind turbines, which sit atop the wildly shaped construction. According to the plan, the wind would supply 8% of all energy in the building. But problems with maintenance and noise levels turned the wind blades into mere decoration. Since then, the building has become synonymous with 'green-washing', whereby architectural designs incorporate elements of green technologies without ensuring they actually work.

LEVC TX5

The electric taxi started replacing its dirty diesel predecessor in early 2018. Now, the biggest challenge for London is to build up new, city-wide infrastructure for recharging.

Toyota Prius

Londoners quickly adopted the Uber app after its launch in 2012, much to the dismay of black cab drivers. Unlike their new competitors, they have to go through extensive training in an attempt to commit London's street network to memory (nicknamed 'The Knowledge').

 (120) **Strata SE1**
BFLS

🕐 2010   📍 SE1 6EE   ↕ 148M

Agusta A109E

This helicopter tragically crashed into a crane working on St George Wharf Tower on a foggy morning in 2013, while attempting to land at London Heliport. The pilot and a pedestrian died on the spot.

St George Wharf Tower (121), or Vauxhall Tower, used similar tactics to ease its way through the planning process, also by placing a wind turbine on top (although this time, only one). The 'glass cigar' was originally rejected by planners but was later approved by the then deputy prime minister, John Prescott. It became the tallest residential tower in London. Two years after completion, *The Guardian* newspaper revealed that two-thirds of the luxury apartments were owned by foreign billionaires, many of them through offshore companies. Some of the names seemed to confirm the fear that London had become a deposit box for dirty money. Although now sold out, the building is practically empty, as most of the owners bought the flats only as an investment purchase or a holiday home.

 (121) **St George Wharf Tower**
Broadway Malyan

🕐 2014   📍 SW8 2AZ   ↕ 181M

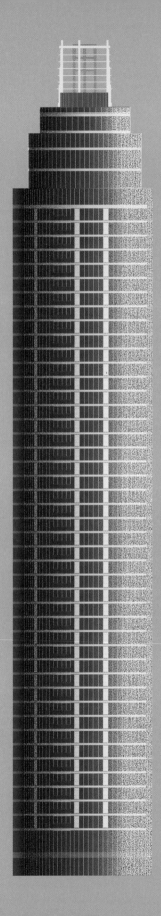

In 2016, Londoners voted in Sadiq Khan as the new mayor – a human rights lawyer who proudly identifies himself as the son of a London bus driver. Quite a change from his predecessor's Eton / Oxford background. To tackle London's long problem with pollution, especially from diesel vehicles, Khan set up the Ultra Low Emission Zone in central London. From 2019, vehicles with older engines will pay an extra fee on top of the Congestion Charge. Controversially, all black cabs are exempt from paying, unlike ambulances or fire engines.

Khan's toughest challenge is definitely the delivery of affordable housing, something both Livingstone and Johnson struggled to do. His new plan supports councils and housing associations in the building of new housing stock. Councils are now forced to rediscover their role as a developer, something that was abandoned four decades earlier (see p.92). Housing can be delivered by as much as a third cheaper when directly developed by the council, cutting out the middle man. There is an increasing number of architects who shun working on commercial projects and now focus on working with the councils.

Peter Barber is one such example; he has delivered affordable housing on different projects all around London. On a small site down a dead-end street in Stratford, he designed a row of terraced houses in association with Newham Council. **Worland Gardens (122)** is a simple yet playful building that pays respect to the surrounding Victorian terraces, while being unmistakeably modern at the same time. These six townhouses are designated as shared ownership, where residents own a part of the house while the council owns the rest. This helps people who can't afford owning the whole house to get their foot on the property ladder.

Worland Gardens
Peter Barber Architects
🕓 2016   📍 E15 4EY

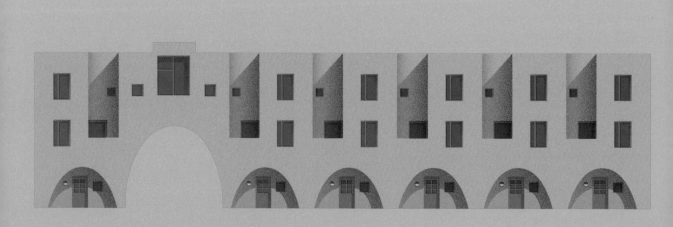

The End

The modern age presented London with multiple infrastructure challenges, but the city always found a way to turn these challenges into opportunities. The result is a melting pot of architectural styles of a scale unseen in most other 'global cities' – from Art Deco to postmodern, and everything in between. And yet, the city has managed to maintain both its character and quirk; the surging tide of constant redevelopment never succeeded in unseating a notorious British love for tradition. And so it follows that you can find a ninety-year-old telephone booth sharing pavement space with an electric car charging station.

In today's age of political and economic uncertainty, London's skyline may seem to have an uncertain future. But as history shows, the city always finds a way to overcome such obstacles. The present housing crisis and lethal pollution levels are pressing issues, but they are arguably dwarfed by the devastating wartime destruction of the 1940s and the toxic pollution levels of the 1950s. London and its cityscape have proved time and time again to remain extremely resilient in the face of adversity and change, and there's little doubt it will stay that way.

↑ 075
↑ 006
↑ 086
001

St. Pancras ⇌
099

088

052

Regents Park ⊖

016

048

054

027

← 033

011

← 071

← 032

Oxford Circus ⊖

047

055

118

041

069

010

056

059

024

090

← 029
← 065

036

060

04

Hyde Park Corner ⊖

Westminster ⊖

049

101

104

067

068
008

Victoria ⇌

← 002

094

085

023

050

019

← 045

046

Vauxhall ⊖

096

072

121

007 ↓

039

005 ↓

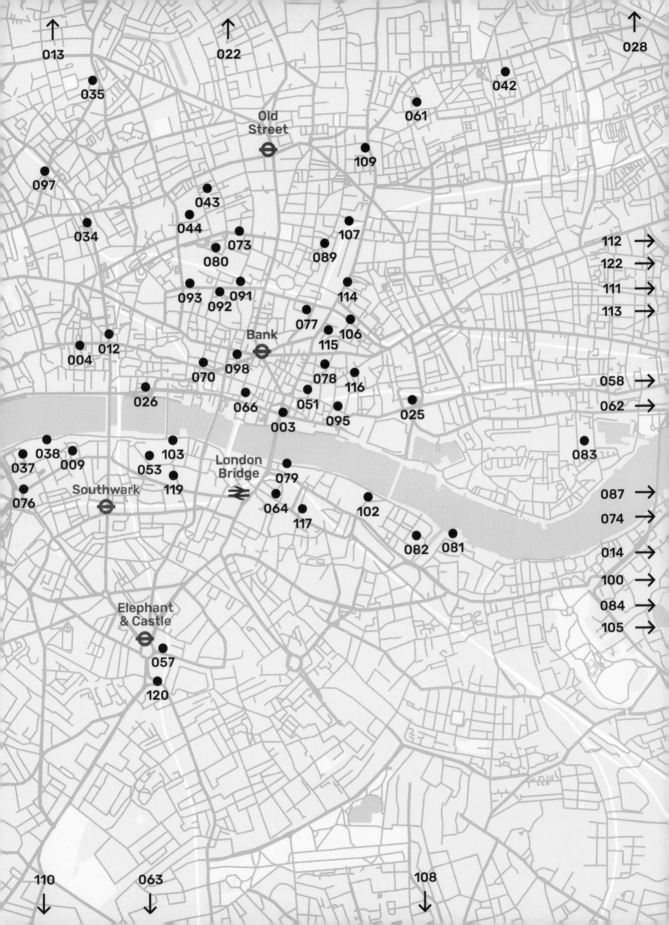

Index of Buildings

Acknowledgements

Further Reading

This book is dedicated to Lilly, the love of my life, who provided me with the inspiration, the energy and the brains needed to finish it.

Thanks to my superb commissioning editor Anna Watson and to Nina Cosford, who put us together. My gratitude also goes to Thaddeus Zupančič, Christopher Beanland and Mark Ovenden, as their extensive knowledge proved invaluable. Thanks too to Glenn Howard for helping with the design. And finally, I'd like to thank to my mum, Marcelik and Vivi for their continued support and overall excellence.

Tom Dyckhoff, *The Age of Spectacle: Adventures in Architecture and the 21st-Century City*, 2017.

Ken Allinson, *Architects and Architecture of London*, 2008.

John Grindrod, *Concretopia: A Journey Around the Rebuilding of Postwar Britain*, 2013.

Cathy Ross & John Clark, *London: The Illustrated History*, 2011.

Mark Ovenden, *London Underground By Design*, 2013.

Nicholas Waldemar Brown & Graham Reed, *London's Waterfront: The Thames from Battersea to the Barrier*, 2003.

Douglas Murphy, *Nincompoopolis: The Follies of Boris Johnson*, 2017.

Rowan Moore, *Slow Burn City: London in the Twenty-First Century*, 2016.

Miroslav Sasek, *This is London*, 1959.

Brimming with creative inspiration, how-to projects and useful
information to enrich your everyday life, Quarto Knows is a
favourite destination for those pursuing their interests and passions.
Visit our site and dig deeper with our books into your area of interest:
Quarto Creates, Quarto Cooks, Quarto Homes, Quarto Lives,
Quarto Drives, Quarto Explores, Quarto Gifts, or Quarto Kids.

First Published in 2018 by White Lion Publishing,
an imprint of The Quarto Group.
The Old Brewery, 6 Blundell Street,
London N7 9BH, United Kingdom.
T (0)20 7700 6700 F (0)20 7700 8066
www.QuartoKnows.com

A catalogue record for this book is available from
the British Library.

ISBN 978-0-7112-3972-2

1 2 3 4 5 6 7 8 9

Typeset in Rubik by Phillipp Hubert
and Sebastien Fischer

Printed and bound in China